First Week with My New iMac

A Very Basic Guide
for Mature Adults and
Everyone Else
Who Wants to
Get Connected

Pamela R. Lessing

Capital Books, Inc.
Sterling, Virginia

Copyright © 2000 by Pamela R. Lessing

All rights reserved. No part of this book may be reproduced or utilized in any form or by any means, electronic or mechanical, including photocopying, recording, or by any information storage and retrieval system, without permission in writing from the publisher. Inquiries should be addressed to:

Capital Books, Inc.
P.O. Box 605
Herndon, Virginia 20172-0605

Notice of Liability

The information in this book is distributed on an "As is" basis, without warranty. While every precaution has been taken in preparation of the book, neither the author nor Capital Books shall have liability to any person or entity with respect to any loss or damage caused or alleged to be caused directly or indirectly by the instructions contained in this book or by the computer software and hardware described in it.

Trademarks

Apple®, iMac™, and Apple Computer® are trademarks of Apple Computer, Inc. Screen shots reprinted with permission from Apple® and AOL®. All other trademarks are used only in an editorial fashion and to the benefit of the trademark owner, with no intention of infringement of the trademark.

ISBN 1-892123-33-9   (alk. paper)

Library of Congress Cataloging-in-Publication Data

Lessing, Pamela R.
   The first week with my new iMac : a very basic guide for mature adults and everyone who wants to "get connected" / by Pamela R. Lessing.
   p. cm.
Includes index,
ISBN 1-892123-33-9 (alk.)
1. Microcomputers. 2. Computer networks. 3. World Wide Web. I. Title.

QA76.5 L4843 2001
004.165--dc21

Book design by Ellen Banker

Printed in Canada on acid-free paper that meets the American National Standards Institute Z39-48 Standard.

First Edition

10 9 8 7 6 5 4 3 2 1

To My Father

Who bought me my first computer
and who now would take great pleasure
in seeing where it has taken me.

Contents

Acknowledgments		vii
Introduction	Read This to Find Hidden Special Offer!	1
Chapter 1	WYSIWYG: Prepurchase or Preassembly Instructions	5
Chapter 2	Out of the Box: What You Should Do Whether Help *Is* or *Is Not* on the Way	9
Chapter 3	Everything Is Connected—So Now What Do I Do?	25
Chapter 4	The First Time: All Alone with the Computer (Will My Family Still Respect Me in the Morning?)	31
Chapter 5	What Is the Internet? What Is a "User Name"? Just Tell Me How to Find Out What the Weather Will Be *HERE*!	41
Chapter 6	The Time Has Come: I Am Really Ready to *DO SOMETHING*	47
Chapter 7	More to the Internet than Just E-mail: The World Wide Web Is Waiting!	63

Chapter 8	Some Simple Basic Fun??? This Is Like the Piano! Do I Really Have to Practice One Hour a Day?	73
Chapter 9	Writing Documents and Correspondence: I Am Already in the Middle of the Book and I Still Don't Know How to Write a Letter!	79
Chapter 10	Everything Else, Including Other Ways to Get Information and Have Fun, or, What Do I Do with All These CDs and Did I Have to Pay Extra for All This Stuff?	99
Chapter 11	A *Step-by-Step* Guide for Each Task	107
Appendices		163
Appendix A	Troubleshooting and the Usual Questions, or, Why Won't This Stupid Thing Work?	164
Appendix B	Some Important Key Commands	177
Appendix C	Some "World Wide Web" Addresses of Interest	179
Appendix D	E-mail Etiquette: "Smileys," Abbreviations, and Other Tips	186
Appendix E	Tech Support: Phone Numbers and Web Site Addresses	188
Appendix F	Healthy Computer Habits: Taking Care of Yourself Physically and Mentally	189
Glossary		193
Index		215

Acknowledgments

My deep appreciation goes to Kathleen Hughes, Julie Kuzneski, Jeannie Hickman, Ellen Banker, and everyone at Capital Books for their expertise, commitment, patience, and understanding. I also thank my illustrator, David Shenton, for once again bringing his own creativity and humor to the text.

I thank Chuck Palmer for his technical help and entertaining explanations. Additional thanks go to all my other friends who delight in sharing their love for the iMac computer along with their special "tips." In particular, I also wish to thank Betsy Friess, who kept me laughing while working very hard as my best proofreader.

My family and friends from around the world were once again encouraging, enthusiastic, and involved in all aspects of this project, and I thank them for their continued support.

I thank Fuma, Zingela, Veni, and Seti for forcing me to take breaks while writing, by swinging a tail in front of the monitor, walking along the keyboard, and resting a head against my hand. It reminded me that the iMac makes a nice warm bed, and that not everyone thinks the computer is the most important thing in life.

Most of all I thank Judith for all of the above and much more.

Introduction:
Read This to Find Hidden Special Offer!

Let's be honest. Most people do not read introductions—especially if it is an informational book and all they want to know is how to do some task. In fact I would guess that most people who buy this book will jump ahead to a chapter heading that looks interesting and just "go for it"! This is in spite of the fact that I have gone to a great deal of trouble to lay out a narrative that follows a simple, logical pathway for working with your new computer. That is fine. I am not offended. I personally never read introductions until I am halfway through the book and realize that there might be some useful information at the beginning of the book that will clarify all these other pages. With that in mind, I shall try to offer an introduction that resembles a good newspaper article and provides answers to the questions: who, what, when, where, why?

Who Is This Book For?

This book is written for my mother and for everyone else, whether they have ever touched a computer or not. It is written for you. You pretend that you will never need to learn how to use computers. You have not grown up with computers, and you are really afraid of the machines. You are also embarrassed that you are not a "computer literate" person. However, what is more important is that you are well-read, have some extra time (and money), have an interest in all that is happening around you, and want to keep in touch.

The problem is that you have heard horror stories of computers "crashing," "viruses," documents "lost" for a variety of reasons, and hours of work gone, etc., etc. You have been told, *incorrectly*, that computers are "much too complicated." Or someone has said, "Why do you want to start learning (playing with) something like this now?"

The answer is, "Why Not???" And as for all the things that can go wrong—this guide will help you learn the techniques to prevent disasters. In truth it is most unlikely you will ever be doing work that is so complicated as to have these things happen. (If you get to this level, you will know how to prevent the problems or have the telephone number for tech support on your speed dial.)

What Will I Learn from This Guide?

Everyone learns in a different way. Also, everyone finds one technique that works best for him or her. **This guide will show you a number of different ways to get your computer to do the things you would like it to do.** It will give you a nice narrative in the beginning, along with helpful tips. More importantly, you will have a simple "one, two, three" guide in the back of the book. This will give you several pages of step-by-step instructions that can be a "quick reference" guide. After all, you cannot be expected to remember all the steps after just doing something a few times. Think of it this way: Important businesses and large corporations have used Chapter 11 to get themselves out of trouble for years. Now you have your very own Chapter 11 to bail you out! (There are also appendices full of helpful information.)

When Can I Start? *or* When Will I Find the Time?

These are two different questions. You can start anytime you want. You might find this book amusing to read even if you are not sure you want to buy a computer now or ever. In fact, looking over this guide might help you decide whether this is a challenge you really want to try. My own feeling is obvious. I would not have gotten my 85-year-old mother a computer if I had not thought she would be able to manage it and enjoy it. In addition, I would not have gone to the trouble of writing this guide if I did not think that this is a skill that anyone can master at any age.

The second question is a bit more difficult. As I point out in Chapter 8, **you will have to practice**. In some ways this is like the piano (but much more interesting)!

In the beginning it will seem to take a great deal of your time. But after a few days, you will find that you are enjoying the time spent on the computer. The Internet will open a whole world of possibilities, and it will be fun to send e-mail to friends and family. Still another advantage of taking time each day to "work" on the computer is that it will improve your hand-eye coordination, improve physical dexterity, prevent arthritis from setting in, and keep your mind active. What a deal!

Where Can I Put It?

You no longer need to buy a laptop computer to save space. The iMac® is a desktop computer that combines the processor (the main computer "brains") and the monitor into one colorful unit. One of the fun aspects about buying an iMac is that you get to choose from a number of bright, vibrant colors. (In fact, with this book in hand, the most difficult part of your computer experience might just be deciding on which color you like best!) Space is really not an issue. Think of all the ways you are saving space: You will no longer need a bookshelf full of encyclopedias, reference books, atlases, and telephone directories. You do not even have to keep the local newspaper to get the movie listing! (Of course, your bookshelf might instead be loaded with computer books like this one!)

Why Should I Be Doing This?

What a silly question! Why shouldn't you be involved with the most interesting communication source that has ever existed? Why shouldn't you be able to get information on any topic that interests you? Think of all the advances that have taken place in your life. While it may have taken you a bit of time to get used to them or know how best to use them, the fact is that you probably do enjoy the remote control for the television, the answering machine for the telephone (not to mention the push-button telephone itself, depending on your age), and many other things that have become a part of your daily life. Age and technical ability are not the issue. Interest and curiosity are!

So now I have gone through the five "Ws," and you are wondering what the "hidden special offer" is. I know that it is difficult to get start-

The First Week with My New iMac

ed, and you may not feel comfortable sending your first few e-mail messages. Therefore, I am offering to answer one e-mail that I receive from you so that you can test your skills. My address is: prlessing@bigfoot.com. I might even send you a terrific joke in addition to responding to your message. Of course, if you want to send me nice comments about the book, it will make me very happy. However, I shall be happy to hear anything you might like to tell me. Perhaps your suggestion might even be included in the next edition!

Here's a list of activities that you should plan on doing during the first week or two with your new computer:

- Send and receive e-mail.

- Search for something on the World Wide Web.

- Play lots of games like solitaire.

- Use a program (such as the *World Book* or *Encarta Encyclopedia*) that's on a CD (compact disk) or just listen to an audio CD.

- Write a letter or document of some kind, save what you have written, and print it.

Please *do not panic* after reading this list. The whole point of this guide is to show you the basic, simple way to do all of these things. So let's get started!

Chapter 1
WYSIWYG: Prepurchase or Preassembly Instructions

The computer term "wysiwyg" (pronounced "wizzy-wig") is an acronym for "what you see is what you get." When you buy an iMac it is important that you understand this. It is terrific if you are reading this book before purchasing your first Apple® computer, because you can follow the checklist below when you go to the computer store. If you have already bought your iMac, you can see if you have everything you will need to get started.

The First Week with My New iMac

Apple Computer, Inc., prides itself on having developed a system that is easy to assemble and easy to use. The iMac is a self-contained desktop computer where the brains of the machine and the monitor (the thing that looks like a television) are a single unit. In addition to this, there is also a keyboard and a "mouse." These are called "peripherals" and they are used to enter information into your computer. When you purchase an iMac, these are the three basic pieces of "hardware" you will find in the box along with several connecting cables. Your computer will also have lots of "software" that is preinstalled. (These are the programs that you need so that the computer knows how to do the things for which you bought the computer in the first place.)

What is NOT included is important. You do not have a way to print out your work. You do not have some way to save or back up your work or to transfer your information into another computer. In addition, you may find that you do not have a truly comfortable mouse and keyboard. Some of these pieces of hardware do not come with any computer, so this is not unusual. However, it is important for you to know this so you can purchase *everything* you will need to get started properly.

The following is a list of the basic items you *should* purchase in addition to the iMac computer:

1. A printer—there are many excellent, inexpensive color printers that will handle most of the tasks you would like to do, including producing excellent photographs with the use of special paper.

2. A printer cable—this is something that is often forgotten, but is essential to connect the printer to the computer so that the two can "talk" to each other.

3. A drive to back up and save the information you have entered into the computer. There are several types of drives—floppy disk drives, zip disk drives, rewritable CD disk drives. Each has its own special advantage ranging from price to amount of information stored and flexibility.

4. Disks—a box of whatever type you will need for the drive you choose to buy.

5. A surge protector—this device prevents excess or irregular electricity from blowing out your new, expensive piece of equipment.

6. A CD with games such as solitaire, Scrabble, chess, etc.—be sure to get one that works on the iMac operating system (OS). They are not at all expensive, and you are buying this computer to have fun! You can always tell people that you are buying them for educational purposes so that you can practice some of the techniques mentioned.

In addition, you should take some time while in the computer store to try using the keyboard that comes with the iMac and the mouse. While many people are very happy with the standard items that come with the basic package, others prefer a larger, ergonomic keyboard and mouse. There are many possibilities, and it is worth spending the extra money for the equipment that fits you the best. After all, you will be spending a lot of time on the computer and it is important that you are comfortable and "set up" properly so that you do not injure your hands, wrists, and neck (see Appendix F).

Keep in mind that the mouse is the hardware or piece of equipment that you will be using the most, so it is very important that it is comfortable in your hand. The iMac operating system is designed to be "user friendly." The idea is that you have lots of "icons" or pictures that represent different tasks. By pointing the mouse cursor, the arrow that moves around your screen or "desktop," at one of these icons and pressing the button on top of the mouse once or twice, you make things happen. In addition, it is by pointing the mouse cursor at something, holding down the mouse button, and moving the mouse that you can move an item to another place, change its size and shape, or highlight it. This is called "clicking and dragging" and is a very important skill that you will need to know to use this computer properly.

The First Week with My New iMac

Please do not worry about all these new terms and the tasks described above. After all, before reading this chapter, you probably thought that the most difficult part of buying an iMac was deciding what color to choose! All of these things are explained as you read along. What is important is that you understand that a mouse has now become a necessary part of your life, and it is important that the two of you are comfortable with each other. By all means start working with the mouse that is provided with your iMac. Just be aware that "mice" come in all shapes and sizes. You can change to a different one if you wish.

Chapter 2
Out of the Box: What You Should Do Whether Help *Is* or *Is Not* on the Way

I know you are excited because the new computer has just arrived. You cannot wait to get *"connected"*—send and receive e-mail, communicate with the grandchildren at school, "surf the Web," check your investments every 15 minutes, etc. Maybe you have a computer because your friends all said it was so much fun playing games and keeping all the correspondence organized. Whatever the reason, this is *important:*

The First Week with My New iMac

While technically the iMac is supposed to be easy to set up, if you have a child, grandchild, friend, or young neighbor who has offered to help you set up your new computer, WAIT FOR HIM OR HER TO COME OVER. DO NOT TOUCH ANYTHING! You have already waited this long—what is a few more hours or days? You can do other things in the meantime like:

- Stock the refrigerator with soda and assorted munchies that this helpful person will appreciate.

- Clear a space where all the new equipment will go. (If you do not have room on a desk, you can buy a special "computer table" for very little money. It will hold everything, and there are many different styles.)

- Make sure that an electrical outlet and a phone jack are nearby. If they're not, you can go out and buy an extension cord for the telephone—and while you are at it, get a surge protector for the computer. (See the list in Chapter 1, and don't worry if you do not know what this item is. Just ask the salesperson at the computer store or the local hardware store. He or she will know.)

If you *must* open the box, KEEP EVERYTHING TOGETHER and DO NOT THROW **ANYTHING** OUT (including the box).

Once you have opened the different boxes, check to see if you have a printer cable to connect the printer to the computer. Remember, these things are like batteries—they are not included! (Also, if you want to be able to have a copy of all the information on your computer, such as correspondence and financial records, see that you have a disk drive and the proper disks to go with it.)

Lift out the iMac and place it on the desk you wish to use. Take out all the cables, the keyboard, the mouse, the disk drive, and the printer. Place everything where you think you will want it to go. Be sure that this is a place where you can sit comfortably and that it has good lighting. Now admire all this wonderful equipment and wait for your helper

Out of the Box

to arrive. Whatever you are thinking, please follow these instructions—they really will save your helper time in the long run, I promise!

If you *do not* have someone to help you, then you should open the box and:

1. Check the list of things to do while you're waiting (above), because it is good advice for you also (especially the part about food and drink, although your favorites might be stronger than sodas!).

2. Check the section above about opening the box. It is important to keep everything together and not to throw anything out!

3. Get out and *read* the quick set-up information that came with your computer. They really do a good job of explaining where to connect each item and how to get started. There will be two booklets with the iMac. The first will show you, in pictures, how and where to attach the different cables. *Before starting this process,* look at the beginning of the second booklet, which tells you the name and location of each outlet, port, and item on the machine. Using both of these guides, you can set up the basic computer. Please note that there is no explanation of how to incorporate a disk drive into the configuration. *In order to do this go to Chapter 11, where this is explained in detail.*

When everything is connected, you will want to turn on the computer. On the front of the monitor (the thing that looks like a television), on the right side, is a small, round button that has the universal power symbol (⏻). Press this button. Then press the similar-looking button on the top right-hand side of the keyboard. The computer is now turned on.

You will hear a "bong" sound and various noises. Just wait while the machine gets itself up and running. You will see the "iMac face" in the

11

"Welcome" box, and then some icons (pictures) will scroll across the bottom of the screen. When more icons (pictures) appear in front of you to the right of the screen and words appear along with a line at the top of the screen (along with the "Apple" symbol and a clock), you will be ready to begin. I suggest that the first thing you do is become familiar with the mouse because this is one of the most important ways that you will communicate with the computer.

Using the Mouse

Take the mouse in your hand—left or right; it makes no difference. The only thing that is important is that the "tail" (or cord) is pointed away from you or "up." Now just move the mouse around and see where the cursor goes. (**Note:** if you have chosen to buy another type of mouse, it will probably have several buttons and even a "scroll wheel." When I say to press the mouse button once [click] or twice [double-click], I want you to press the *left* mouse button. Do not touch the right mouse button. You do not need it right now.)

The cursor will look like an arrow, large letter "I," or hand, depending on where it is on the desktop or in an open window. Don't worry. The different looks are signs to you that the cursor can do different things. For example, when you are working with text, the cursor can be your

Figure 2.1

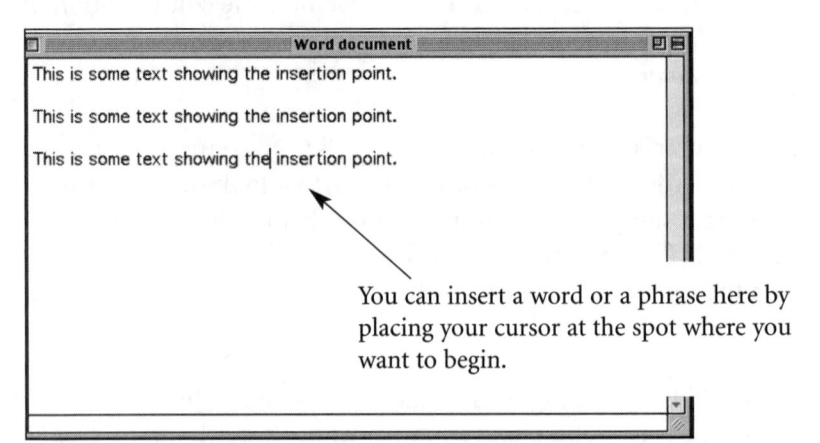

Word document
This is some text showing the insertion point.
This is some text showing the insertion point.
This is some text showing the insertion point.

You can insert a word or a phrase here by placing your cursor at the spot where you want to begin.

Out of the Box

"insertion" point. If you want to add a word or phrase in the middle of a line, you place the cursor at the spot where you want to begin. Then you press the mouse button once (click). There is now a blinking "I" in that spot and it shows that this is where the words will appear when you start typing. More on this later! (See figure 2.1.)

Notice that you do not need to stretch your arm all the way to the kitchen to move the cursor to the far corner of the computer desktop. If you are near the edge of the mouse pad, but the cursor is not yet over to that icon in the upper right-hand corner, physically pick up the mouse and place it back in the middle of the mouse pad. Then start moving it again. (Go ahead and try this now. You see it is the ball under this contraption that is causing the cursor to move. When it is not in motion, nothing happens. Hold the mouse in one hand and place your other hand on the ball on its underside. With your finger, roll the ball around and look at the monitor to see where the cursor is moving.)

Your hand should be holding the mouse lightly and you should be comfortable. You should also be able to reach the button at the top of the mouse with your index and/or middle fingers. After you have gotten used to moving the mouse around, you have two ways of practicing the skills you will need to operate the computer. I strongly suggest that you go immediately to the "Help" menu at the top of your screen and follow the very good "tutorial" that the people at Apple have provided. It will teach you the names of different things and teach you how to do very important tasks. Most importantly, this tutorial is interesting and a lot of fun! I have also written out some exercises that will help you to learn how to use your mouse. If you like, you can follow my directions in the section **Practicing with the Mouse** and then do the tutorial later. The order in which you do this does not really matter, but I *strongly* suggest that you do both.

The First Week with My New iMac

Mac Tutorial on Using the Mouse

Move the mouse cursor so that it is pointing on the word "Help" on the gray bar at the top of your screen or desktop. Press the mouse button once (click). Notice that the word "Help" is now in a colored box and the letters are white, not black. A menu of optional tasks has now appeared in a list below. You are viewing your first "drop-down menu."

Hold down the mouse button and drag the mouse down the list until you highlight the term "Mac Tutorials." Press the mouse button once (click). A window will "open" and in the middle of the window will be several items written in blue. Point the mouse cursor on the one that says "Desktop Skills" and press the mouse button once (click). The screen will go blank temporarily, and then the tutorial will begin. Read each of the "pages" and follow the directions. I am sure you will be amused by their approach and patience. (When you are slow to do something or cannot find a word, the computer will "draw" a red circle around the area to show you where you need to go. Wouldn't it be nice to have something like this in our everyday lives!) When you are all done you can point the mouse cursor on "exit" and press the mouse button once (click) to leave the tutorial.

Practicing with the Mouse

You should now be comfortable with moving the mouse around randomly. Next you need to try "dragging" an item to another area of the desktop (the screen in front of you). To do this, point the mouse cursor on one of the icons and hold down the mouse button. While holding down the button, start to move the mouse left and right or up and down. When the icon is in another spot, release the mouse button. Congratulations, you have just learned (or are practicing again) one of the most important skills you will need to operate your computer! This is called "clicking and dragging."

The icon is now positioned in a different place. Go ahead and do this "clicking and dragging" a few times. Do not worry if you have trouble getting the icon to the spot where you would like it to be the first time.

Out of the Box

This is just practice and later in the book there is a really fun way to perfect this skill (see chapter 8).

Opening and Closing Windows

Practice "clicking" or pressing the mouse button by pointing the cursor (the arrow, hand, or large "I") on an icon and pressing the button once (clicking) or twice (double-clicking—two rapid clicks). Then relax your death grip on the mouse! If everything is lined up correctly, you will have opened *something*. It really does not matter what. The reason it does not matter is that you will also learn how to "close" that window since you do not need it for this exercise.

Whatever has just opened has a bar running along the top of the window with horizontal lines and a name or "title" of the window in dark letters. The dark letters and the horizontal lines show that this is an "active" window—that you are working with it. This line is called the "title bar." It is important to remember that name, because your grandchild (or friendly helper) may refer to it when giving you instructions over the telephone. At the extreme left of the title bar (the dark horizontal lines) is a small square. Point the cursor inside this box and press (click) on the mouse button once (see figure 2.2).

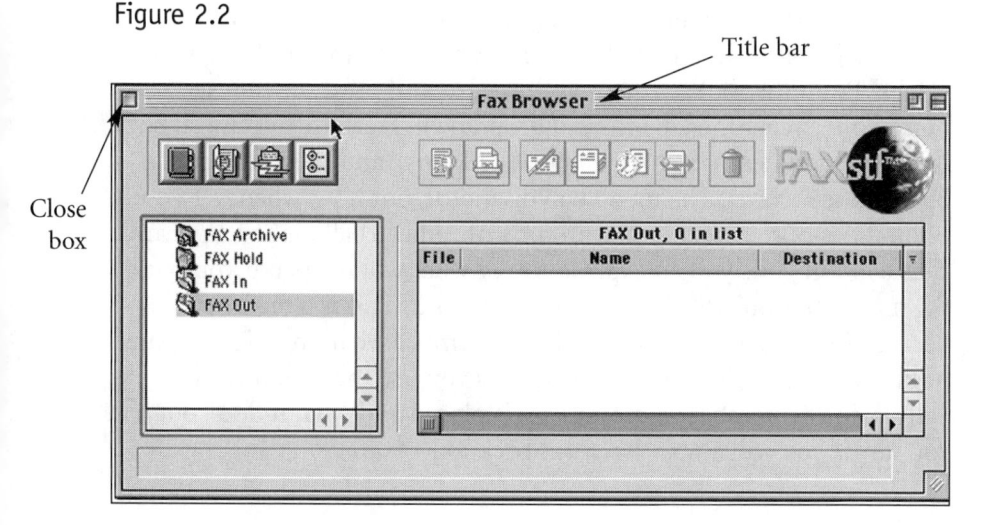

Figure 2.2

15

The First Week with My New iMac

Now the window is gone! Knowing how to open and close windows is probably one of the most important lessons you will learn, so practice this a few times. There are other ways to close a window or program, and they will be discussed later. In addition, you will learn how to change the size and position of a window by following the tutorial and/or the directions in a later chapter.

Now that you know how to move the mouse around a little bit, let's make it easier to see everything on the desktop. In addition, let's make it easier to understand what each of these icons does and to what each of these words refers.

Finding Help

As you look around the screen (desktop), you will see lots of words and pictures. While the meaning of some of these may seem obvious, there are many that you will not recognize. Also, it will be hard for you to understand all the uses of each item. If you point the mouse cursor on one of these words or icons and a balloon appears with a description of that item, terrific!

However, if this "Help" feature is not turned on, this is what you need to do to make your first week (or perhaps your first month) easier. On the left side of the top line is the Apple symbol [] and five words. This line is called the "menu bar." The word all the way to the right says "Help." Point the mouse cursor at this word and press the mouse button once (click). A "menu" will drop down. Point the mouse cursor on the second item which says "Show Balloons," and press the mouse button once (click). The menu will disappear, but now, whenever you point the mouse cursor on a word or icon, a little balloon will appear. This balloon gives you an explanation of what will happen if you press the mouse button (click) on that icon or word. This is a big help because it means you do not need to remember what every icon means or how every icon is used. I know that as you use the computer, you will start to remember where an icon is placed and what it does, but if you forget you will always have this backup.

Out of the Box

Another way to get help is from the "Help" menu that comes with every program. As stated above, it sits with other words, not icons, on a light gray line at the top of your desktop, and is called the menu bar. (Remember, on the left of this bar you will always see the Apple symbol [] and on the extreme right side you will have the name of the program within which you are working or the "Finder" icon. More on this later.) Note that if you go to the "Help" menu before starting any program, you have a special feature, the "Help Center." By opening this item you can have some of your basic questions answered as quickly and directly as possible (see figure 2.3).

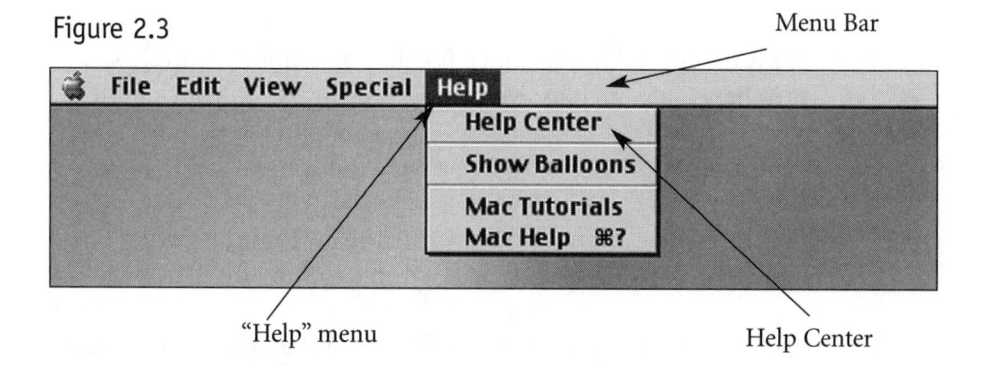

Figure 2.3

"Help" menu   Menu Bar   Help Center

Making Everything Easier

Next you will want to make everything easier to see and easier to use. There are several ways to do this.

Look at the bottom of your desktop (the screen in front of you) and notice that there is a gray bar of icons or pictures at the bottom. This is the "Control Strip," and each icon stands for an item or setting you can change or adapt on the computer (see figure 2.4).

Figure 2.4

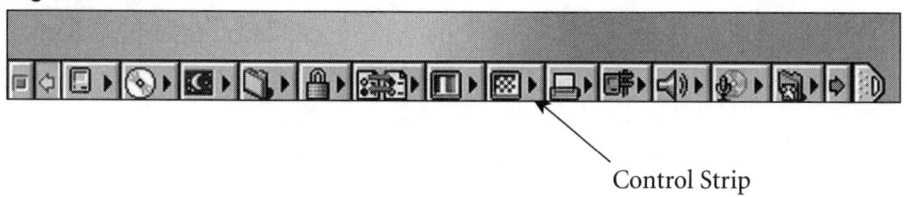

Control Strip

17

The First Week with My New iMac

If the Control Strip is fully extended 13 icons will be visible.

1. To make everything larger and easier to see:

   - Point the mouse cursor on the eighth icon from the left—the one that looks like a checkerboard—and press the mouse button once (click).

   - Point the mouse cursor on the lowest number you see, which should be "640 x 480, 117Hz," and notice that it is now "highlighted."

   - Press the mouse button once (click) while pointing to these numbers and watch as everything is enlarged on your desktop!

2. To make the sounds from the speakers louder:

   - Point the mouse cursor on the third icon from the right, which looks like a speaker with sound coming out of it.

   - Press the mouse button once (click) and then point the mouse cursor on the box that is positioned inside the slide of the volume control.

   - Hold down the mouse button and slide the control up or down to change the sound level.

Another way to make changes is to go to the "menu bar." Look at the top of your "desktop" and notice that there is a gray bar with the Apple symbol and a row of words. Once again, this is the "menu bar." To change some settings to your preferences you will need to go to the "Control Panels" (see figure 2.5).

To open the Control Panel, point the mouse cursor on the Apple symbol and press the mouse button once (click).

Out of the Box

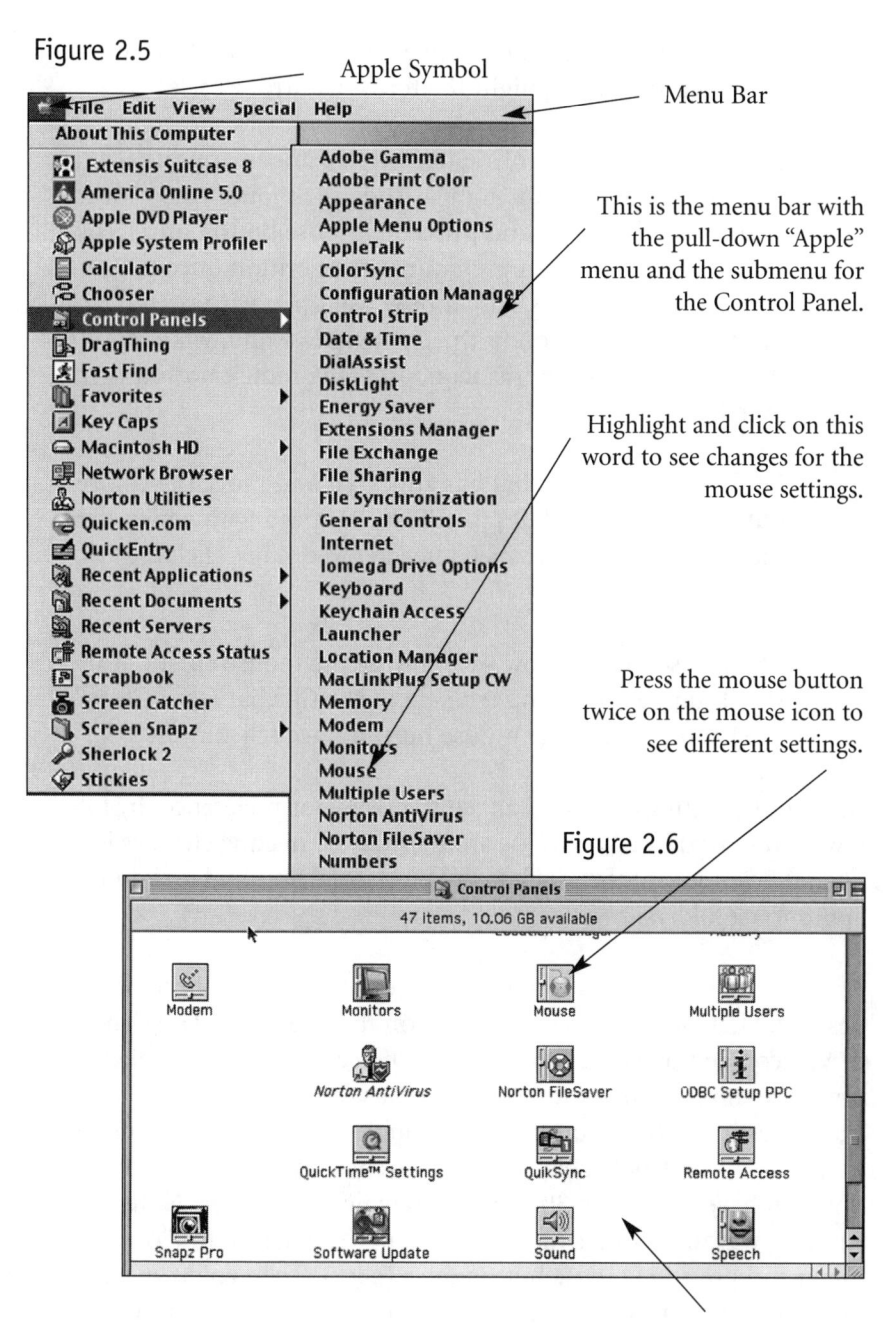

Figure 2.5 — Apple Symbol — Menu Bar

File Edit View Special Help

About This Computer

- Extensis Suitcase 8
- America Online 5.0
- Apple DVD Player
- Apple System Profiler
- Calculator
- Chooser
- **Control Panels** ▶
- DragThing
- Fast Find
- Favorites ▶
- Key Caps
- Macintosh HD ▶
- Network Browser
- Norton Utilities
- Quicken.com
- QuickEntry
- Recent Applications ▶
- Recent Documents ▶
- Recent Servers
- Remote Access Status
- Scrapbook
- Screen Catcher
- Screen Snapz ▶
- Sherlock 2
- Stickies

Control Panels submenu:
- Adobe Gamma
- Adobe Print Color
- Appearance
- Apple Menu Options
- AppleTalk
- ColorSync
- Configuration Manager
- Control Strip
- Date & Time
- DialAssist
- DiskLight
- Energy Saver
- Extensions Manager
- File Exchange
- File Sharing
- File Synchronization
- General Controls
- Internet
- Iomega Drive Options
- Keyboard
- Keychain Access
- Launcher
- Location Manager
- MacLinkPlus Setup CW
- Memory
- Modem
- Monitors
- Mouse
- Multiple Users
- Norton AntiVirus
- Norton FileSaver
- Numbers

This is the menu bar with the pull-down "Apple" menu and the submenu for the Control Panel.

Highlight and click on this word to see changes for the mouse settings.

Press the mouse button twice on the mouse icon to see different settings.

Figure 2.6

Control Panels — 47 items, 10.06 GB available

Modem | Monitors | Mouse | Multiple Users
Norton AntiVirus | Norton FileSaver | ODBC Setup PPC
QuickTime™ Settings | QuikSync | Remote Access
Snapz Pro | Software Update | Sound | Speech

This is the Control Panel with several icons displayed

19

The First Week with My New iMac

- Drag the mouse down the alphabetical list of applications and folders until you highlight the term "Control Panels."

- Notice that a new list of items or a new menu appears. To change the speed of the mouse, slide the mouse cursor down to the word "Mouse" and press the mouse button once (click). (Alternatively, you can press the mouse button once on the word "Control Panels." A window will open with several icons. Find the "Mouse" icon in the new window and, while pointing the mouse cursor on this icon, press the mouse button twice.) (See figure 2.6.)

- Look at the window that has appeared and move the colored button on the two slides to adjust the speed with which the mouse moves and the speed needed to double-click the mouse.

- Then close this window by pointing the mouse cursor at the small square on the top left side of the title bar (the "Close" box) and pressing the mouse button once (clicking).

Many other settings can be changed to meet your preferences by following the steps listed above OR another way of making changes is to open the window of the Macintosh HD (hard drive) and look in the appropriate folders.

As an example you might want to change the color or pattern of your desktop. First, point the mouse cursor on the Macintosh HD (hard drive) icon and press the mouse button twice (double-click). Next, point the mouse cursor on the folder that says "System Folder" and again press the mouse button twice (double-click). Then find the folder that says "Control Panels" and double-click on that icon. In this window you have more than 30 icons from which to choose! (**Note:** Another way to do this is to point the mouse cursor on the "Apple" menu and press the mouse button once [click]. Then go down and highlight the term "Control Panels" and click once. Now you see the

Out of the Box

same window as the one above. Still one more technique—using just keyboard commands—is explained in Chapters 4 and 11.)

DO NOT PANIC, just highlight and open the top item that is called "Appearance" by pointing the mouse cursor on this icon and pressing the mouse button twice (double-clicking). Then click on each tab and see all the adjustments that you can make to customize your desktop. (To make adjustments in this window you will need to use several different techniques. For some tabs, such as "Themes" and "Desktop," you need to either:

- point the mouse cursor on the colored slide button and hold down the mouse button as you move the slide button left and right; *or*

- point the mouse cursor on the arrows on the side of the scroll bar and hold down the mouse button to "scroll" through the options.

For other tabs, you need to point the mouse cursor at the item and press the mouse button once (click) to see what options you have. Still others need to be "toggled," which means they are made "active" or "inactive" by clicking in the box by the item to check it (active) or leave it blank (inactive). Finally, close this window by pointing the mouse cursor on the small box on the title bar in the top left corner of the window and pressing the mouse button once (clicking). (See figure 2.7.)

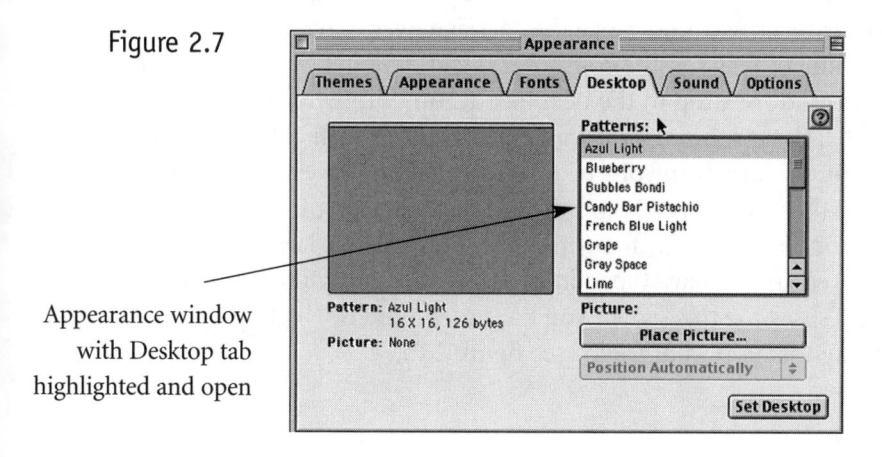

Figure 2.7

Appearance window with Desktop tab highlighted and open

21

If you want you can try opening some of the other icons that seem relevant and see what changes would be interesting for you. (Also note that, in addition to the "Control Panels," the System Folder has a folder that is labeled "Control Panels (Disabled)." However, changing to disabled settings is a bit complicated and you will want to have someone come in and do this for you.)

Now, if you have made a number of changes, congratulations! You have accomplished a great deal and you should take a break and get yourself something to eat and drink. If you have not been able to make these changes please remember that none of these is essential. They are mentioned so that using the computer is easier and fun for you. (You might want to wait and try doing these changes another time while following the directions in Chapter 11; this approach might be easier for you.) Also, this is the moment you might consider hiring someone to come over and set up all the basics that are described in this chapter and the next. It is *worth the money*!

The Keyboard

If you are used to using a typewriter, then a number of things on your new computer keyboard will look familiar. However, some of the keys work differently from those on your old typewriter. So even if they do look similar, you will need to learn to use them in other ways.

An example is the "**return**" key, which is in the same position, has the same name, and looks like the "return" key on your typewriter. On the typewriter this key would move the carriage over, allowing you to type the next line of text. On the computer it is different, because the words "wrap around" or drop to the next line automatically, and you do not have to tell the machine to start a new line of text. The return key on the computer does drop your text down one line (for example, when you want to start a new paragraph). However, it also can act like a shortcut or command for the computer. Pressing this key is like saying "go find" when you have typed in a Web address. It is also like saying "OK" or "show me this" when you have identified or "highlighted" something that you want to do (see figure 2.8).

Figure 2.8

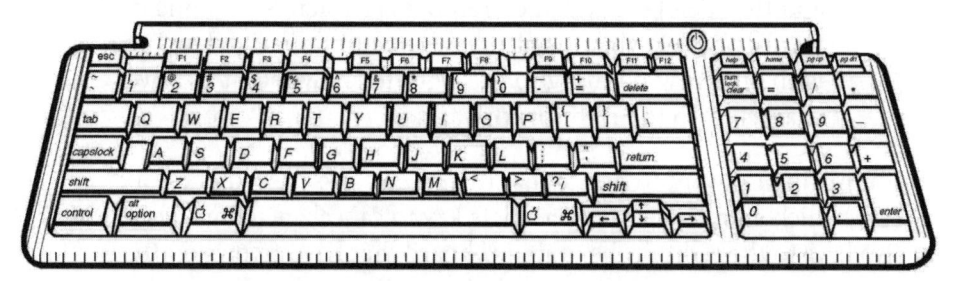

Everything will be much clearer when you have some idea of where different keys are and what some of the new keys are called. Some examples:

- Find the key that has "**control**" on it. It is on the bottom row of the keyboard, all the way on the left. The "control" key is used as a shortcut for a variety of tasks; for example, it will bring up a "contextual" menu for a folder or application. Point the mouse cursor on the folder, hold down the "control" key, and press the mouse button once (click) to see this menu.

- Find the key that has "**alt**" or "**option**" on it. This is the "alternate/option" key. This key is to the right of the control key and helps you find optional characters on the keyboard. Examples are accents for foreign languages, Greek symbols, or scientific notations. You do not see these characters displayed on your keyboard, but they are available to you if you learn which keys to press.

- The next key has the Apple [] and also a "⌘." There are two of these keys on either side of the long "space bar." This used to be called the "**Apple**" key (for obvious reasons) and is now known as the "**Command**" key because that is its function. It allows alternative ways to get the computer to do your tasks by using keys as shortcuts.

23

The First Week with My New iMac

- Check where the "**tab**" key is as you will be using this a lot, and the "**delete**" key, which removes characters by going backwards. Some keyboards also have an additional "**delete**" key with an arrow pointing to the right to show that it removes characters to the right or forward.

You might also want to notice that there is an "**esc**" key (the "escape" key), which allows you to use a single key to cancel an action. There are also keys to the right of the main keyboard that have arrows on them and allow you to move the cursor in four different directions.

If you have trouble finding these different keys, go ahead and look at figure 2.8 on page 23. I know there are lots of other new keys that you are wondering about, but you will not need them right away. This guide is to help you with your early days on the computer. So very simply put, if I do not mention it in this book, DON'T TOUCH IT YET!

Chapter 3
Everything Is Connected—
So Now What Do I Do?

So the computer is sitting in front of you and if you have a wonderful helper, he or she has raced through all the steps to "install" whatever the helper thinks you need. In addition, he or she has probably been really efficient and registered all your new equipment. If you do not have anyone to help, this is not a problem. There are detailed instructions in this book explaining how to do all of the things mentioned below. Just turn to Chapter 11 and get started.

The First Week with My New iMac

Here are some things that you will need to know and do. If you have a helper who is *really* nice, please ask him or her to:

- Show you the different ways to turn the computer on and to shut it off (see end of chapter).

- Show you where and how to put in and take out CDs and how to use the floppy, zip, or rewritable disk drive that you may have chosen to purchase separately.

- Slow down the mouse, make fonts bigger, and enlarge the size of the "windows" (see figure 3.1).

Figure 3.1

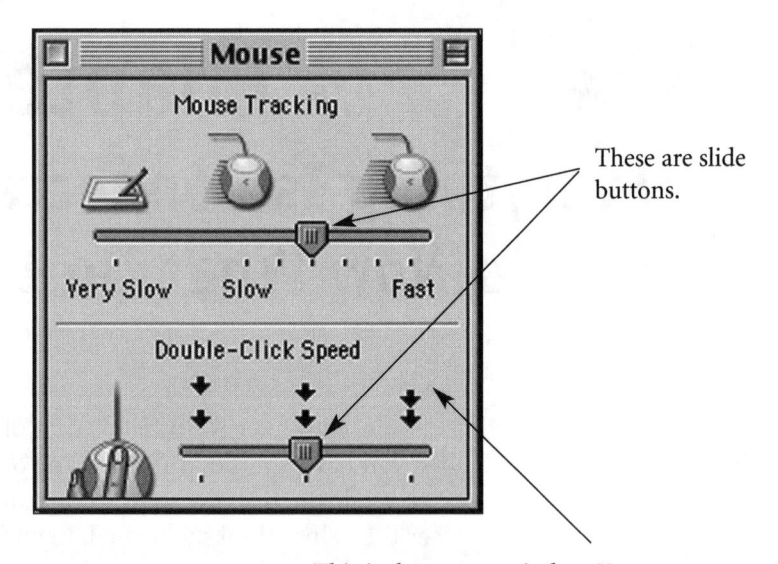

These are slide buttons.

This is the mouse window. You can control the speed at which your mouse operates by clicking on the appropriate speed, or by moving the slide button to the left.

- Get you signed on with an Internet Service Provider (ISP) and help you pick out your user name and "password."

Everything Is Connected

- Set up an "address book" with all the e-mail addresses of family and friends. (Also ask your helper to put together a "buddy list" while you have him or her here and happily working for you.)

- Make sure you have a folder on your desktop that is called "My Documents." Also have your helper add to that folder several other new folders with names like "Correspondence," "House," "Car," etc. (Don't forget to have folders with the names of all your kids and that favorite grandchild who is helping you put all this together!)

- Show you how to open, move, resize, and close windows.

- Set up a "template" with your letterhead and a fax letterhead. (If your helper really knows what he or she is doing and has the time, or is willing to come back. This might depend on whether you have good snacks.) Your helper can then also set up which "font" and what color lettering you would like to use for all your correspondence.

- Put the shortcuts for your Internet Service Provider, your letterhead, and a few games like solitaire on your desktop.

- Make sure all written work is automatically saved to a new folder called "My Documents" as a "default" so that none of your work is lost.

If you do not have a wonderful, helpful person with you, DO NOT PANIC! Go to Chapter 11 for all the information on how to do these things. Also do not panic that you do not know the meanings of lots of the terms I have just used, like "default" and "fonts." They are really unimportant for now and were only mentioned with the thought that you might have a person sitting there ready to help you get started. (However, this is a good time to mention that you should keep a notebook by the computer so you can write down any questions you have. Some of your questions may be answered in the back of this book, but

27

The First Week with My New iMac

some may not. By writing things down, you can ask someone for help or perhaps e-mail the question to a friend or to me. That way I will know what I have left out and need to add in the next edition!)

A term that you *do* have to know is *"desktop."* The screen in front of you looks like a television, but is usually called a "monitor." Where you normally see only one big picture on your television, your desktop has lots of little pictures of things or "icons." You will also have several things that my mother calls "frames" and that the industry calls "windows" (see figure 3.2).

Try to think of the screen in front of you as the desk at which you sit in your office or study. On your desk you have your telephone to the right and your address book next to it. On the left you might have a box with bills that need to be paid or a folder with letters to be answered. You leave the middle area of your desk clear so that you have a place to do your work.

Figure 3.2

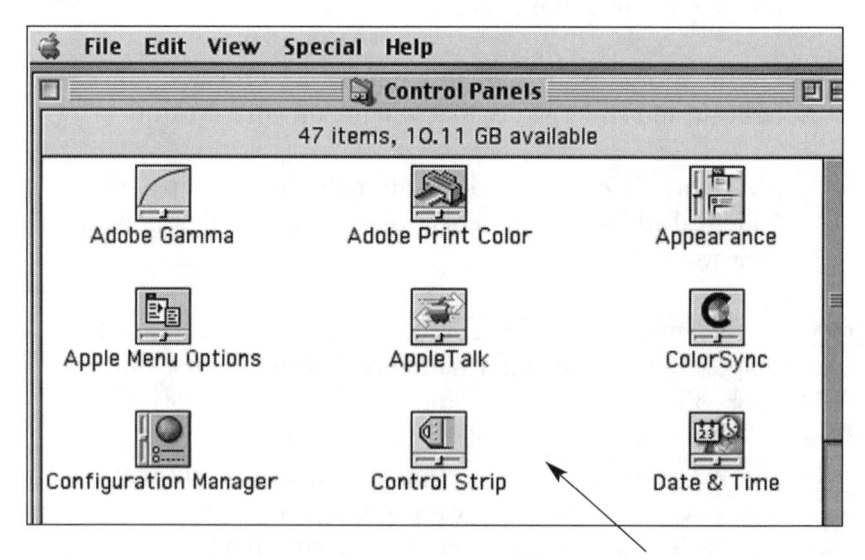

This shows the desktop with icons and an open window.

What Is the Internet? The screen in front of you is just like the desk at which you sit. It is called the "desktop." On the desktop you have different things that you can work on, or play with, that are depicted as "icons" or pictures on the right side. In the middle area you have a place on which to do your work as soon as you have opened up these folders or games. In the previous chapter you practiced opening and closing these folders and moving them around. So now what do you do with these open programs and folders? That question is answered in the next chapter.

Some Thoughts on Turning the Computer On and Turning the Computer Off

Computers operate differently from other electrical equipment. You do not need to "shut down" the computer every night. It is not like the television, the iron, the coffeemaker, or the air conditioner. It will not blow up, burn out, use too much electricity, or hurt anything. The machine is designed to "stay on" in a "sleep" mode. When it is "sleeping" the light on the front of the monitor will turn amber and fade in and out, almost like the machine is breathing deeply or snoring. Yes, the machine will feel hot and your cat will enjoy sleeping on top of it, but it is all right—light bulbs get hot, too. (If you do go away for several days, it is a good idea to turn it off. However, it can stay on day after day just waiting for you to come and play with it.) The step-by-step guide for turning the computer on, turning it off, and restarting it is in Chapter 11 (page 107).

Chapter 4
The First Time: All Alone with the Computer (Will My Family Still Respect Me in the Morning?)

This is that special moment. You are excited, but also a little anxious. Maybe you have read some books on the subject, or maybe you thought it would be better just to experience everything as it comes. (Well, I guess the latter can't be true if you are reading this, but you know what I mean!) You might also be thinking that this is the worst moment in your life. How could you be so stupid as to spend this amount of money on something you will never figure out?

The First Week with My New iMac

The *most important* fact you need to know is that you cannot break anything by just pushing some of the keys. You may open up a whole lot of windows that you do not want; you may have everything "freeze" (nothing seems to work—mouse, keys, etc.); or everything may go blank as the whole thing "crashes."

BUT, DO NOT WORRY! First of all, you have not put any important information into the computer, so you have nothing that can be lost. Also, if all else fails, you can just turn off the computer with the power button on the upper right side of the keyboard, the power button on the monitor, or the small reset button on the side of the monitor. That allows you to restart the computer and just try again. You may get a nasty message from the computer that you did not shut it down properly, but you are all alone, so you are the only one who knows you made it unhappy. Anyway, it is a machine, and you are the boss. (Although it should be noted that it will act like a two-year-old and refuse to do things at times because it says that it can't. But, unlike a two-year-old, it is telling the truth, and you may need to stop and figure out why it will not do what you want it to do.)

This may also be the moment that you wish you had hired some computer expert to come in and give you lessons. To be honest, you will need to have someone give you lessons at one point. However, the idea for this first week is to get you moving with your new computer and not to be overwhelmed by the 13-year-old who is pushing keys faster than the speed of light. It will also give you a chance to figure out what questions you have, so that you do not feel you are wasting time and money when the teacher arrives.

By the way, this may be a good time to mention that I suggest that you *do not* give your computer a name. It will only empower the machine in your mind, and your family and friends may become jealous when you start spending all your time with Jim or Judith and speak of him or her with greater affection than you ever did any of them.

Before we *really* get started, you will need to understand some terms and try once again to practice a few of the techniques or moves that you will need to get the computer to do what you want. Please understand that there are several ways of doing the same task. It is similar to skiing in that there are always several ways to come down the mountain. (Even an expert skier likes to take easier trails or shortcuts sometimes.) Some people will find all the techniques easy, and others will need to try alternate approaches. Some people find it easy to move the mouse all over the desktop and think this is better than remembering "commands" or special keys to press. Others may have trouble using the mouse at first because they have arthritis or tremors, or have a hard time seeing where they are pointing the "cursor." It is a skill that will develop quickly, no matter how difficult it seems in the beginning. (I am still amazed at how quickly my elderly friends managed to get the mouse "under control"!)

Once you have tried several methods you will know which one is best for you. To make this book easier for you to use, whenever possible I shall give the instructions for using both the mouse and the keyboard commands to perform different tasks. Each method will be clearly labeled. This means that if you know you want to use keyboard commands, you will know when this is possible and then combine the two methods to perform a task.

Using the Mouse

In Chapter 2 we talked about how the mouse actually works and started to practice "pointing," "dragging," and "clicking." Remember as you hold the mouse, the only thing that is important is that the "tail" (or cord) is pointed away from you or "up." Once again, just move the mouse around and see where the cursor goes. In addition, point the mouse cursor on an icon or folder on the right side of the desktop and hold down the mouse button. Now drag the item to some other spot and release the mouse button. Point the mouse button on another icon and press the mouse button once to highlight it. Now press the mouse button twice to open the program or folder. While you do this please remember that your hand should be holding the mouse lightly and you should be comfortable.

The First Week with My New iMac

What you will notice is that the cursor will look like an arrow, large letter "I," or hand, depending on where it is on the desktop or in an open window. It means that the cursor can do different things. As an example look at the document in figure 4.1.

Figure 4.1

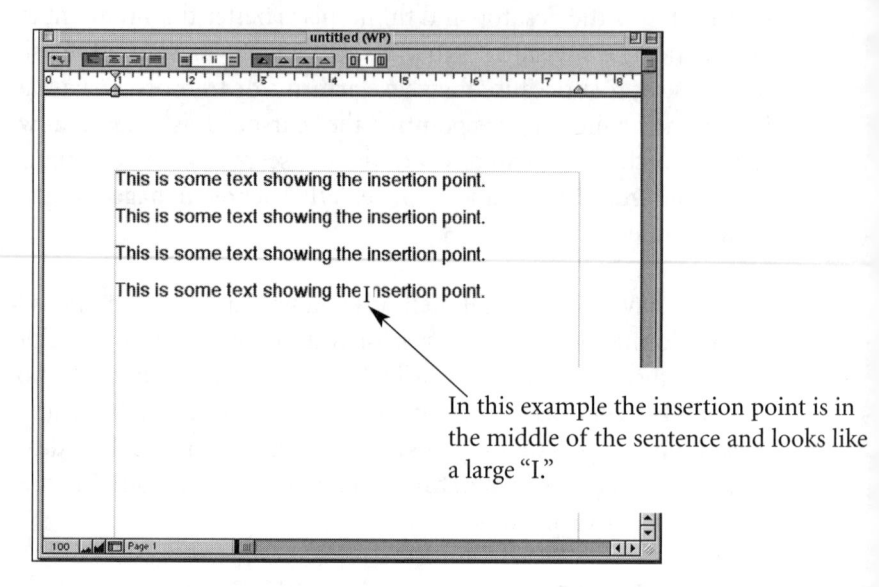

In this example the insertion point is in the middle of the sentence and looks like a large "I."

Menus and Other Shortcuts

That brings us to another way to move around the desktop, folders, or files without using the mouse. These are shortcuts and commands that are not just for the arthritic, but are used by the experts to get things done quickly.

As the first example, when you look at your desktop you see several icons. Use the arrow keys to move around the desktop to highlight different folders or applications (also known as programs). Now try something different. Instead of using the arrow keys, just type the first letter of the first word of one of these icons, such as the letter "S." Is the magnifying glass of "Sherlock®2" highlighted? Try another letter like "T" and see how the Trash can is now highlighted. By highlighting a

The First Time

folder or program, it can easily be opened by pressing the "Command" key and the "O" key (⌘+O).

You can use this same technique once you have opened a folder containing several files or folders. Pressing the first letter of a folder's name will take you to that folder immediately. Using the arrow keys will let you move around the window until you find what you are looking for. The last keyboard command is then the "Command" key and the "O" key (⌘+O) to open the item.

Look at figure 4.2 below. You see an open window on the desktop. At the top is the name of the program you are using, or the folder that is open. (Remember, this is shown as black letters on a horizontally striped line and is called the "title bar.") Above that at the top of the desktop you have one or more lines that are called "bars." One bar will have icons and the other will have words. Look at the gray bar with the words. This is the "menu bar." It is from these menus that you can ask the computer to do some task, such as printing your work, saving a note into a specific folder, changing the size and font of a document, etc.

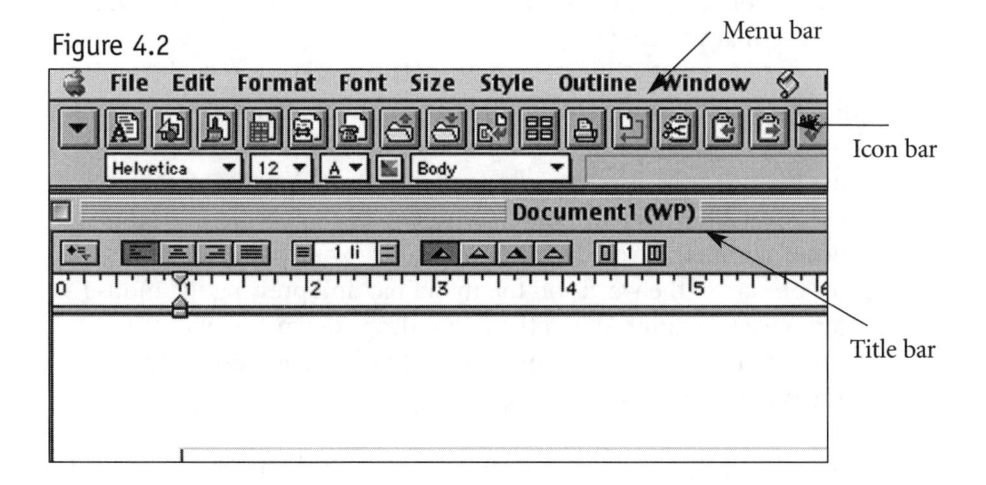

Figure 4.2

Menu bar

Icon bar

Title bar

35

The First Week with My New iMac

So, how do you get the menu to drop down and give you choices? If you point the mouse cursor on one of these words and press the mouse button once (click), a drop-down menu will appear. Now you have a lot of possibilities—words and commands that are written in black. (You will also see some words that are written in gray, not black. They are "shaded" and hard to read. These are choices that are not available to you at this time. More on this later.)

To the right of some of these words you will see the "Command" symbol and a letter. This is a "key command" or shortcut that you can use to perform some task. For example, if you want the computer to "Save" or "Print," you just press the "Command" key and the "S" or "P" key simultaneously, then release them to execute that command. For many of these commands you will then see another box that will ask you a few questions to complete your request/command. This is a "dialog" box. However, if you pressed the "Command" key and the "Q" key (simultaneously), it is telling the computer that you want to close this program. It is like pressing the mouse button (clicking) on the small square box on the top left of your window (the "Close" box). (Note that the "Command" key and the "Q" key will close or end that program, while the "Command" key and the "W" key will only close that window.)

While it is nice to learn some of the basic key commands, it is certainly not necessary. The iMac operating system was designed to use the mouse because it is "user friendly" and fairly easy. You can combine mouse commands and keyboard commands. In fact, when you forget a keyboard command, you can always "find it" by pointing the mouse cursor on one of the words on the menu bar and pressing the mouse button once (clicking). When the menu drops down, you will see a key command to the right of many of the tasks. (For a list of key commands and shortcuts see Appendix B.)

As an example, if you are playing a card game like solitaire, you would start by pointing the cursor on the solitaire icon on the desktop and pressing the mouse button twice (double-clicking). Then you would have an open window on the desktop that would show your playing

The First Time

area and a game that is dealt and ready to play. That is great, but what if you want to play a variation of this game or want a new deal? Then what?

Notice that there is a menu bar above your active window, a gray line with several words on it. If you point the mouse cursor on the "File" menu and press the mouse button (click), a drop-down menu appears. Notice that there are several choices, including "New Game," "Start Over," "Close" (meaning just this window), and "Quit." If you press the "Command" key and the "N" key (⌘+N) simultaneously and then release them, the cards for the next game will be dealt. If you want help, go to the Options menu and then press the "Command" key and the "H" key (⌘+H) simultaneously (and then release). A description of how to play the game will appear (see figure 4.3).

The First Week with My New iMac

Figure 4.3

Menu bar
Title bar

In this game, the Options menu will give you the "help" instructions.

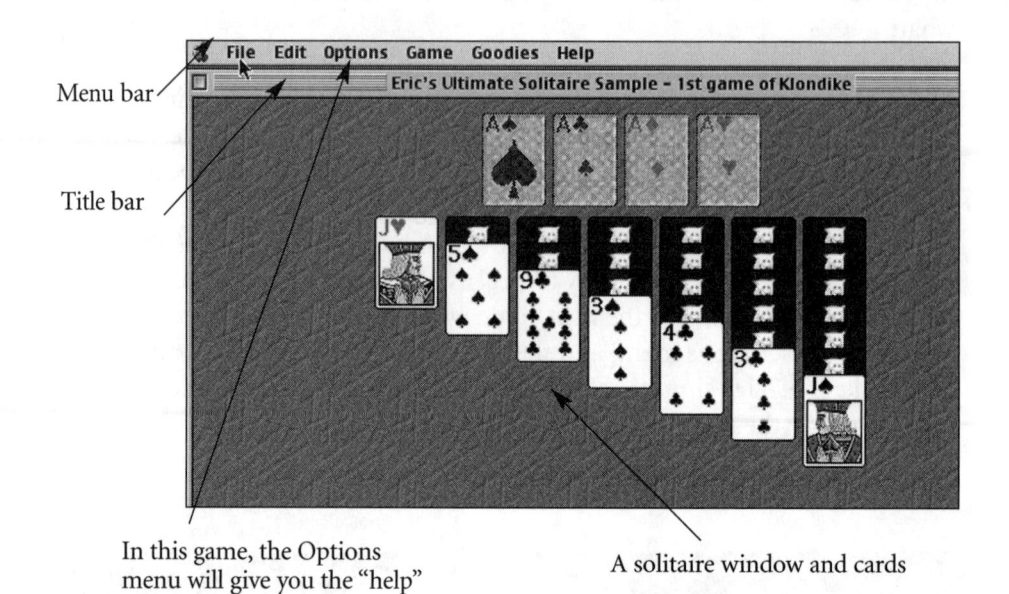

A solitaire window and cards

In addition, there are other important keys that you can use to execute commands, including the "return" key and the "arrow" keys. When you are asked a question in a dialog box, or need to tell the computer to go ahead and do something, press the "return" key to say, "OK, do this." (Think of the remote control for your television. When you press "Enter" it is like saying, "Yes, I want this channel." "Return" is the same as "Enter.")

The arrow keys are useful for many things. They can move the cursor to different spots on a letter or document that you are writing. They can also "scroll" (move) down a section of the e-mail that you are reading. That way you do not have to hold down the mouse button on the arrow symbol at the bottom of the scroll bar. (The scroll bar is a vertical bar on the right or a horizontal bar on the bottom of an open window. It is active when a window is too small to show all the available information. By clicking on the appropriate arrow, more data is visible. For scroll bars see figure 4.4. Also see Chapter 11.)

Figure 4.4

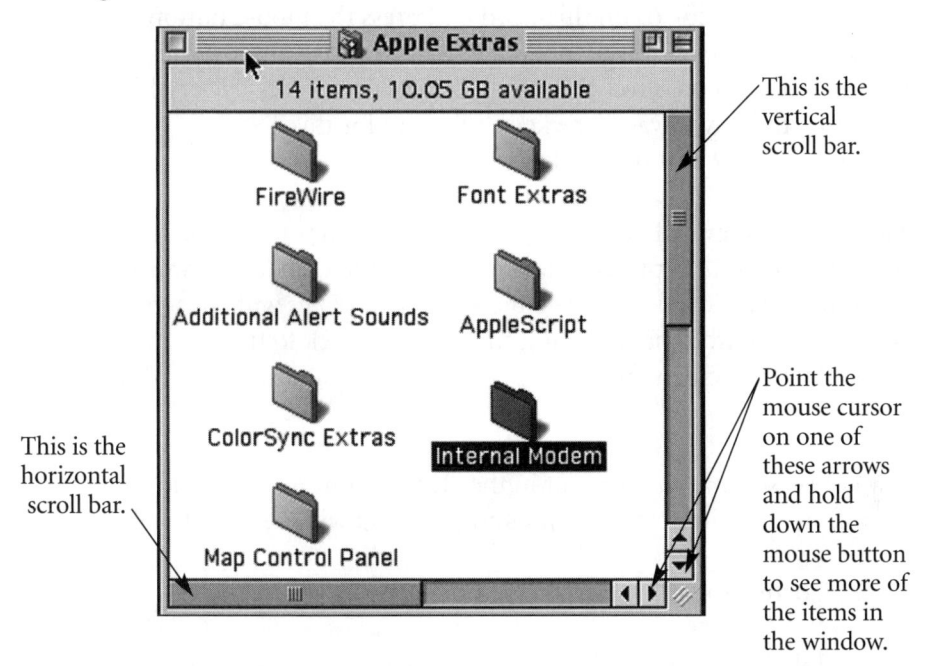

[Figure 4.4: A screenshot of the "Apple Extras" window showing 14 items, 10.05 GB available, with folders for FireWire, Font Extras, Additional Alert Sounds, AppleScript, ColorSync Extras, Internal Modem, and Map Control Panel. Labels point to: "This is the vertical scroll bar.", "Point the mouse cursor on one of these arrows and hold down the mouse button to see more of the items in the window.", and "This is the horizontal scroll bar."]

Arrow keys can also help you "highlight" a word, sentence, or page of text. All you need to do is use the arrow key to move the cursor to the beginning of the word/sentence/page to be highlighted. Then hold down the "shift" key and use the arrow key to move the cursor to the end of the word/sentence/page. Finish by releasing the "shift" key. Now that area is highlighted, and there are all sorts of things you can do with a highlighted area! **Note:** You can also lose the highlighted area if you are not careful. So *be careful*. **DO NOT** press "Backspace" or "Delete." (See **"Undoing" the Damage** below.)

"Undoing" the Damage

There are two remedies if you make a mistake, but you must correct your mistake *immediately*.

The First Week with My New iMac

Keyboard Commands: Do you see the word "Edit" on the menu bar? Point the mouse cursor on this word and press the mouse button once (click) to drop down this menu. Highlight the term "Undo Typing" at the top of the menu. Press the mouse button once (click). Everything is now back the way it was. (The key command for this is the "Command" key plus the "Z" key [⌘+Z].)

Mouse Commands: If you prefer using the icon or button bar, from the left find the 12th picture. (It is near the middle under the word "Outline.") The icon looks like a piece of white paper with an arrow curving backward. That is what it means—"go back to the way things were." Point the cursor at this icon and press the mouse button once (click).

Both of these approaches result in the "Undo" command. "Undo" is one of the most important commands that you will ever use. It will:

- Correct the mistake you just made.

- Take you back to whatever was on your page originally if, after making a correction or change in formatting, you now decide you do not want that paragraph to be bold, italicized, or underlined.

- If you make a mess editing your work or you are now three pages off because your cat walked across the keyboard, it will take everything back to the original.

Don't you wish we could do this in real life?

Chapter 5
What Is the Internet? What Is a "User Name"? Just Tell Me How to Find Out What the Weather Will Be *HERE*!

So everyone is talking about the Internet. Every television show, magazine, and advertisement directs you to the "World Wide Web" and offers you "information." Your question is, "How does this work, and what does it mean to me?"

The First Week with My New iMac

The Internet is a series of interconnected computer systems and services that is worldwide.

Try to think of the Internet as our country. In our country there are cities, and in each city there are buildings. Each city has a different function or job. One city just handles commercial affairs, so it is given an address or name that is ".com." Another city is responsible for all the educational facilities, so its name is ".edu." Still other cities have names like ".net," ".org," ".gov," etc., and each one of these names stands for the type of thing that city does.

Within each city there are buildings, and each one of these is the name of a particular company, school, organization, or network. This is also called the "domain name."

What Is the Internet?

For example, one of the better-known U.S. government agencies is the National Oceanographic and Atmospheric Administration. It issues weather reports along with lots of other interesting information. It is a part of the government of the United States, so its Internet address is: www.noaa.gov. A college will have an address that is the name of the school followed by ".edu"; Ithaca College is www.ithaca.edu. National Public Radio, a non-profit organization, can be reached at www.npr.org. A popular commercial address is www.bn.com, the on-line store for the bookseller Barnes & Noble.

Now, within each "building" there are individuals or areas that you will want to contact. After all, you really do not want to communicate with just anyone at National Public Radio, or Ithaca College, or NOAA and the Department of Commerce. The "user name" refers to the specific person or area that you want to go to inside this building.

As an example, your child named Joan gets her "e-mail" (electronic mail) from the server called "Juno." This company lives in a "building" called juno.com and your child has decided to use her initials as her user name. Her e-mail address would then be jcl@juno.com. (The "@" sign means "at.") If e-mail is sent from one individual in a "building" to someone in the same "building," it is usually not necessary to put in the name of the "building" (Internet Service Provider). You only need to put the user name in the "Send To" box. Think of it this way. The manager of your building knows everyone who lives and works in the building. He does not need to be told that Betsy, Jane, David, Raoul, or Susan lives there. He only needs to know that you want to send your message to Betsy, Jane, and Susan or to David and Raoul. (You can also send it to all of them at once!)

Perhaps you would like to try to use the Internet to find something useful such as the movies that are playing in your area. If you use America Online (AOL) as your Internet Service Provider (ISP), the easiest way to get this information is to "sign on" to AOL. Then go to the third line down from the top of the window. Look for the box that

The First Week with My New iMac

says, "Type Search words, Keywords or Web Addresses here." (It is just below the line with lots of icons in colored rectangles; see figure 5.1.) Type in the word "movies" or www.bouldermovies.com. (I have used my hometown as the example. You need to type in the name of your

Figure 5.1

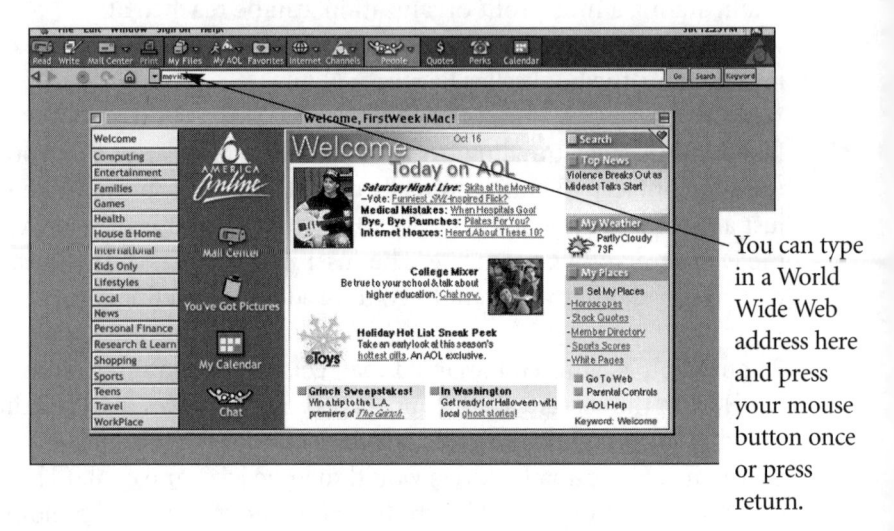

You can type in a World Wide Web address here and press your mouse button once or press return.

city and then the word "movies" followed by ".com.") Detailed instructions on how to do all this are in Chapter 11.

You also might want to know how to get today's weather in your own area or anywhere in the world. If you use America Online as your ISP, whenever you "sign on" there will be a window in front of you that will offer all sorts of instant information (along with telling you if you have received any e-mail from your best friend!). If you point the cursor on the spot that says "My Weather" (the right side in the middle of the window) and press once on the mouse button (click), it will give you a complete forecast for your area. You can then choose Regional, National, or even the weather around the World!

Another way to get this information is to go to the third line down from the top of the window. Look for the box that says "Type Search

44

What Is the Internet?

words, Keywords or Web Addresses here." (It is just below the line with lots of icons in colored rectangles.) Type in the word "weather" or www.noaa.gov or www.weather.com. Then press the "return" key. (You have probably figured this out, but "www" stands for World Wide Web and usually needs to go in front of the Internet address. However, as the technology changes, many addresses no longer need the "www" prefix. I suggest you use it anyway, just to be sure.)

In any case, always type in the "address" exactly as it was given to you. YOU MUST BE PRECISE! DO NOT ADD SPACES. DO PLACE PERIODS (.) AND FORWARD SLASHES (/) EXACTLY AS DIRECTED. If you do not, the computer gets very unhappy and will refuse to take you to the Web site that you want to reach.

Chapter 6
The Time Has Come: I Am Really Ready to *DO SOMETHING*

First Question: What is it that *you* would most like to do with this computer?

The First Week with My New iMac

For most people the answer is that they want to know how to send and receive e-mail. Creating and printing out documents is usually less of a priority—after all, you can still write letters by hand. Assuming that you, or your helpful young person, have set up an account or "trial account" with one of the Internet Service Providers (ISPs) like America Online, Juno, ATT, or Microsoft Network you can get started very easily. (If this is still to be done, see **Setting Up an ISP Account** at the end of this chapter.)

For convenience, I shall use America Online (AOL), version 5.0, as the example when describing all the different ways to use e-mail and to connect to the World Wide Web. I do this for a number of reasons, but not in any way to endorse one service over another. Remember that each of the Internet Service Providers will give you a free trial period. This means that you can "sign on" with AOL (or another service) for 250+ hours and get used to doing basic tasks and then try another ISP to see if that one works better for you.

Getting Connected

The first thing you will need to do is tell the computer that you want to work in the program AOL. The way to do this is to "open" it.

There are several ways to do this:

1. If you or someone else has placed the ISP America Online on the desktop, the easiest is to point the cursor on the icon that looks like a triangle in a blue box on the right side of your desktop and has the words "America Online 5.0" under it. With the cursor on the icon, press the mouse button twice (double-click). (If you have bought a multibutton mouse, remember we are only using the *left* mouse button for now.) If you do not have the "shortcut" on your desktop, go to the next step.

2. Another way to open your ISP is to go to the icon at the top right of your desktop that looks like a rectangle and says

The Time Has Come

"Macintosh HD" under it. Point the cursor on this icon and press the mouse button twice (double-click). When this window opens, use the arrow keys to move down to the icon that looks like a folder with a globe on it and has the word "Internet" under it. Point the mouse cursor at this icon and press the mouse button twice (double-click). In front of you are the names of several Internet Service Providers (ISPs). (See figures 6.1 and 6.2.)

Figures 6.1 and 6.2

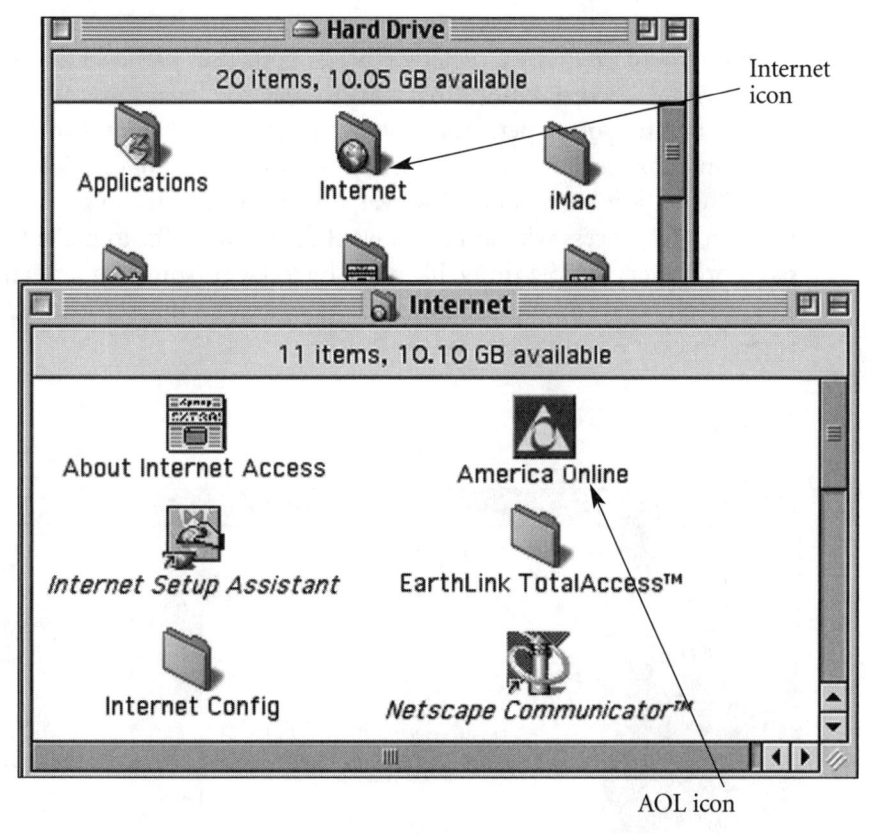

Hard Drive window showing 20 items, 10.05 GB available, with Applications, Internet, and iMac folders. Internet icon labeled.

Internet window showing 11 items, 10.10 GB available, with About Internet Access, America Online, Internet Setup Assistant, EarthLink TotalAccess™, Internet Config, and Netscape Communicator™. AOL icon labeled.

The folders are placed alphabetically, so find the folder that says "AOL" (a blue square with a turquoise triangle in the middle) and highlight it

49

The First Week with My New iMac

either by pointing the cursor on it and pressing the mouse button once (clicking), or by using the arrow keys to get to it. When that folder is highlighted, press the mouse button twice (double-click).

Congratulations! You have opened the program that will lead you to the Internet. *You are about to become connected!* Look at figure 6.3. Notice that there is a window in the center of your desktop that has gray horizontal lines running along its top and the word "Welcome" in black letters. Along the left side of the window is a vertical rectangle with the America Online logo. In the middle of the window there are several rectangular gray boxes. If everything has been set up properly, you will see your user, or screen name in the center of the window. In addition, there might be a rectangle below your user name so that you can enter a password. Enter the password that you have chosen. (You or your helpful young person can set up your account so that your user name and password run automatically and you do not have to enter this information every time. However, if you prefer, you can go through this process whenever you want to sign on.) Try to make the password a very simple thing, like your birthday or your maiden name, so it is really easy for you to remember. Also make a note of it somewhere, in case you do forget it.

Figure 6.3

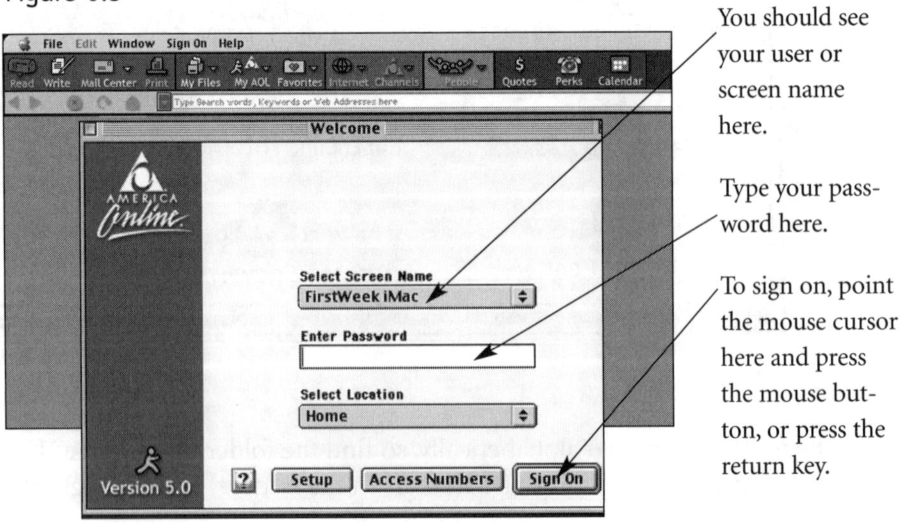

You should see your user or screen name here.

Type your password here.

To sign on, point the mouse cursor here and press the mouse button, or press the return key.

50

The Time Has Come

Another thing to notice is that on your desktop you now have three bars running horizontally across the top. The first one is the menu bar. It is a gray line with words that correspond to drop-down menus. Also note that the name of the program, "America Online," is in the upper right corner of this bar. The next two are toolbars. These bars have several colored rectangles with lots of icons. These icons help you to do different functions. There is also a gray rectangular box in which you can type Web addresses or key words to search for things on the Internet.

If you look back at the "Welcome" window you will see several "buttons" at the bottom of the window. One has a double border around it, which shows that it is the primary choice. This rectangular "button" has the words "Sign On" in it.

Now point the cursor on the button and press the mouse button once (click) or just press the "return" key.

Now wait!

Continue to wait.

I mean it; just wait as the modem connects with the ISP.

This can take a bit of time because your computer's modem is dialing up a special telephone number and trying to get recognized. Sometimes the modem will have to dial two numbers before it connects. (Note that the computer uses your telephone line to connect to the Internet. Unless you have a second telephone line, this means that while you are "on-line" you can't make or receive phone calls.)

While you are waiting you can:

- Listen to the sounds the modem makes.

- Look over the glossary of terms in the back of this book.

51

The First Week with My New iMac

- If you have a second telephone line, call up your children or friends and tell them you are about to send them e-mail if this stupid machine really works.

- Look at the next diagram, which will prepare you for your next "Welcome" window.

Reading and Sending E-mail

Once you are connected to AOL, a new window will appear and a voice will say, "Welcome." If someone has sent you e-mail the voice will also say the famous line, "You've Got Mail!" If no one has sent you any e-mail, make a note to call all your friends, children, and grandchildren and tell them that you are going to a great deal of trouble, time, and expense to move into the 21st century. You expect them to cooperate (read: humor you) and send some mail with which you can practice! Don't forget to tell them what your e-mail address is (see **Your E-mail Address** at the end of the chapter).

The window looks like figure 6.4 and is called the "Welcome window". There are just one or two things about it that are interesting to notice right now. The most important is to find the thing that looks like a mailbox. It sits inside a blue vertical rectangle on the left side of this new window. If there is a yellow square in it and the red flag is up, this is the sign that you have received e-mail. Move the cursor over to the mailbox icon and press the mouse button once (click). (Another way to see that you have mail is to look at the top right corner of your desktop. In the square with the name of the active application, America Online, there will be an icon of a mailbox that alternately flashes with the AOL logo.)

A new window will open that will look like figure 6.5. The title bar will have your user name and say, "Online Mailbox." Notice that the "New Mail" folder in front of you will show a date, a user name, and a subject. The top "piece" of mail will be *highlighted*. To read this e-mail you can either point the cursor on the message and press the mouse button

52

The Time Has Come

twice (double-click) or just press the "return" key. (Remember, the "return" key is like saying, "Yes, I want this." And yes, there are other ways to read your e-mail, but these two are the easiest for now.)

Figure 6.4

This is the AOL's Welcome Window.

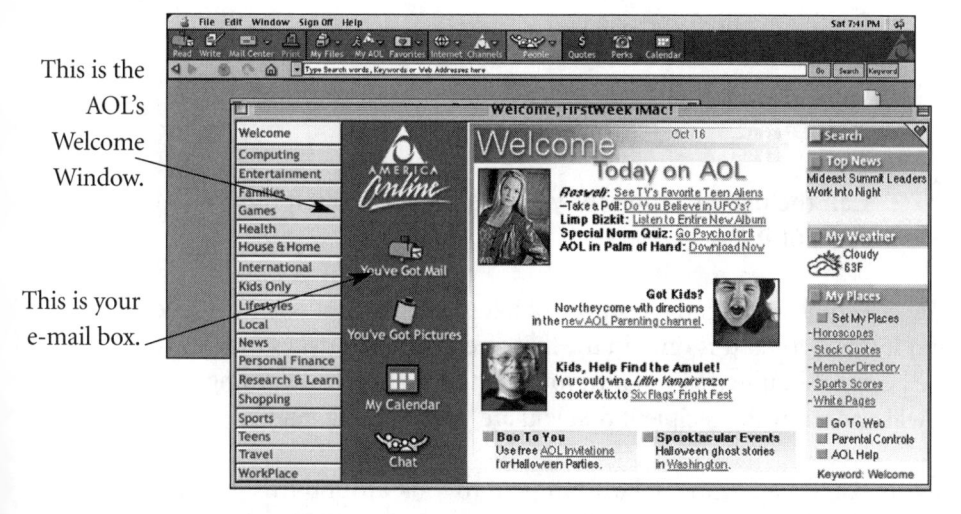

This is your e-mail box.

Figure 6.5

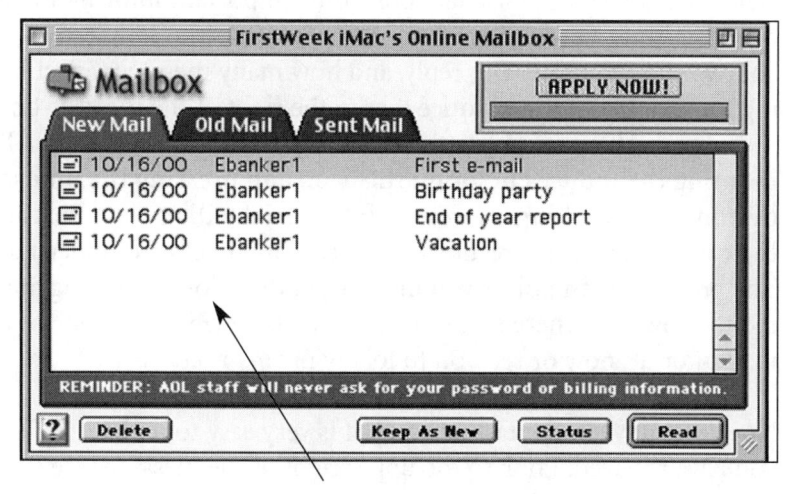

This is the mailbox window when you are online. You can see four new e-mails and the top piece of e-mail is highlighted.

53

The First Week with My New iMac

Congratulations again! You are now reading your first e-mail. Now you have to decide what you want to do. You have several choices:

- Reply to the e-mail.

- Read your next message.

- Go and get something to drink—you have accomplished a major task!

- Call the person who sent you this e-mail and tell him or her you got it!

The last choice defeats the purpose of having e-mail, but you are excited and it is fine to do this once in the first week. A better idea is to reply to the person, because this will give you practice writing and sending e-mail. It will also show the recipient that you are "computer literate."

Before you do anything, take a moment to look around this window and familiarize yourself with all the information available. Notice especially that above the "message" box, some important information is repeated. You can see when the e-mail was sent, who sent it, the address you might need to reply, and how many messages are still waiting for you. In addition, notice that to the right of the message box there is a trash can to delete messages, and there is a "Help" icon. **By pointing the mouse cursor on this icon and pressing the mouse button once (clicking), a wonderful tutorial will appear.** Pick any topic and follow the directions. The prompts are easy to understand. The program even points you in the right direction by circling areas in red to show you where to go to perform a task! (Either do one of the e-mail tutorials now or read on to follow my instructions.)

Now let's move to the task at hand. It is very easy to reply to the e-mail you have received. Look to the upper right of the message (see figure 6.6); there are several icons in a vertical row. The top one says "Reply," the next says "Forward," and the bottom one says "Delete." Move the cursor to the top icon that says "Reply" and press the mouse button once (click). You should now have a new window (see figure 6.7).

Figure 6.6

Subject

Your e-mail message is here.

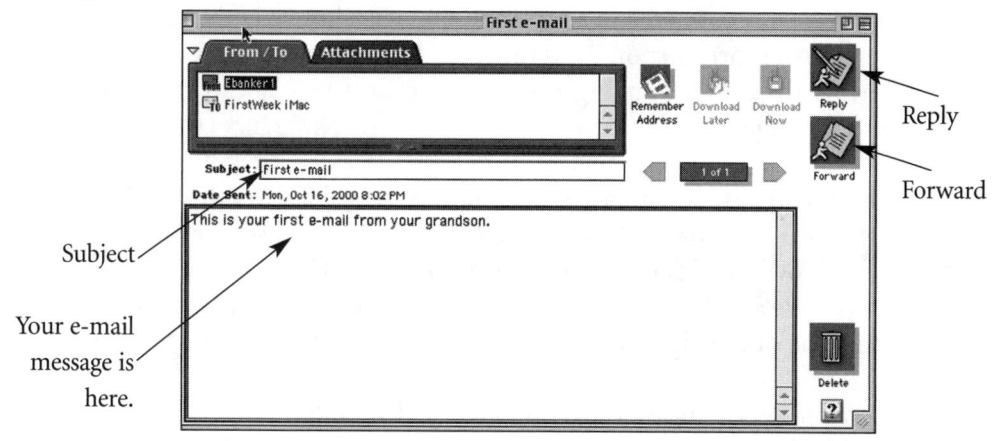

Reply

Forward

Figure 6.7

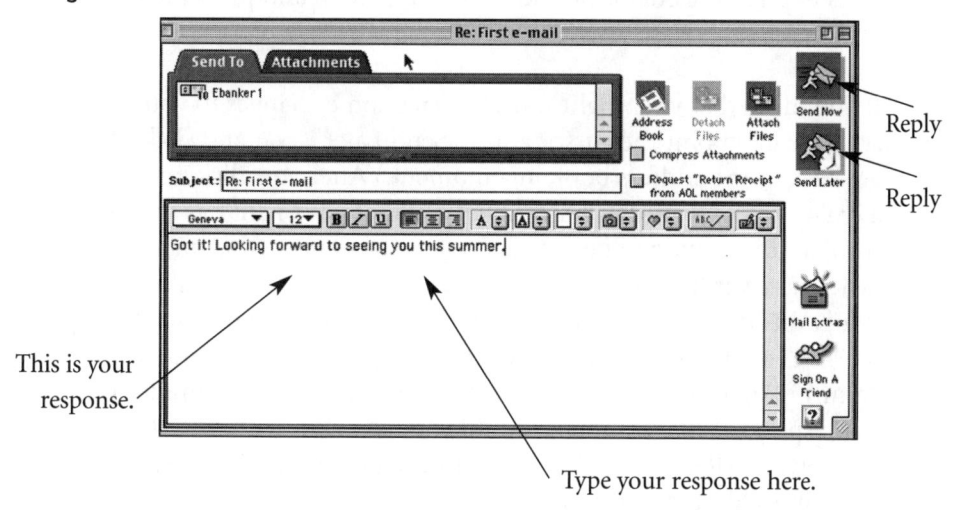

This is your response.

Reply

Reply

Type your response here.

This is your "piece of paper" on which to write your return note. Notice that all the work has been done for you. The "Send To" box already has the correct e-mail address. The "Subject" box refers to the subject of the note the person sent to you. The large box below this is the area that you will use to write your note. Best of all, the cursor is already blinking in this box so that all you have to do is start typing

The First Week with My New iMac

your response. (Some people, like my mother, have trouble seeing the blinking cursor. There is a simple test that will show you that the cursor is in the correct spot. Press the space bar several times. You should now see the cursor blinking in the message area.) Go ahead and type your message.

You should also note that the icons in the vertical line on the upper right have now changed (see figure 6.7). The choices you now have are "Send Now" and "Send Later." Between the "Send To" box and the large icons there are three small icons. One is "Address Book." (Don't worry about the others right now—you really don't need them for a while.)

After you type your message, you need to send it to that person. Just writing the message is not enough. Most of the time, the best thing to do is to place the cursor on the "Send Now" icon and press the mouse button (click).

If you think that you might want to make some changes to your message you can point the cursor at the "Send Later" icon and click. (I will get back to the address book in a moment.) After you click on the icon, a dialog box will appear that will tell you that your mail has been sent (or that it is waiting to be sent). You *must* respond to this message. In fact, whenever the computer asks you a question or tells you something, you *must* respond by moving the cursor to the box and clicking on "OK" or "Cancel." Another way of doing this is by pressing the "return" key, or pressing "Y" for yes or "N" for no. The computer will not respond to any commands until you have answered its statement or question. (Remember, I told you in Chapter 4 that the machine is sometimes like a two-year-old!)

After you have acknowledged that your outgoing mail has been sent, the original message that was sent to you will appear again. Now you have another choice to make. You might want some friend or family member to read the message that you just received. If that is the case, look at the right vertical icons, place the cursor on the second icon that says "Forward," and press the mouse button once (click).

The Time Has Come

The new window in front of you looks different from the one you just used for your reply (see figure 6.8). What has just happened? The computer has copied the message that was sent to you and is ready to send this message on to another person or group of people. All you have to do is fill in the "Send To" box, write something in the "Subject" box, and add a brief comment in the message box. (You can also change the "Subject" box.)

It really helps to add a message so that the person to whom you are forwarding this mail knows why you are sending it. A short message like: "Allison and Jason, thought this would amuse you" or "Augustus, I never knew she would say such a stupid thing," will indicate that you meant to send this on and that you did not just push the wrong buttons.

Now all you do is move the cursor to "Send Now" or "Send Later" and press the mouse button once (click). You will not see the message that you have decided to forward. You will only see your additional message. Do not worry, a copy really is forwarded to whoever you indicated. You will have to press the "return" key to acknowledge that the mail has been sent and then you will see the original message again.

Figure 6.8

Click on one of these buttons to send your message.

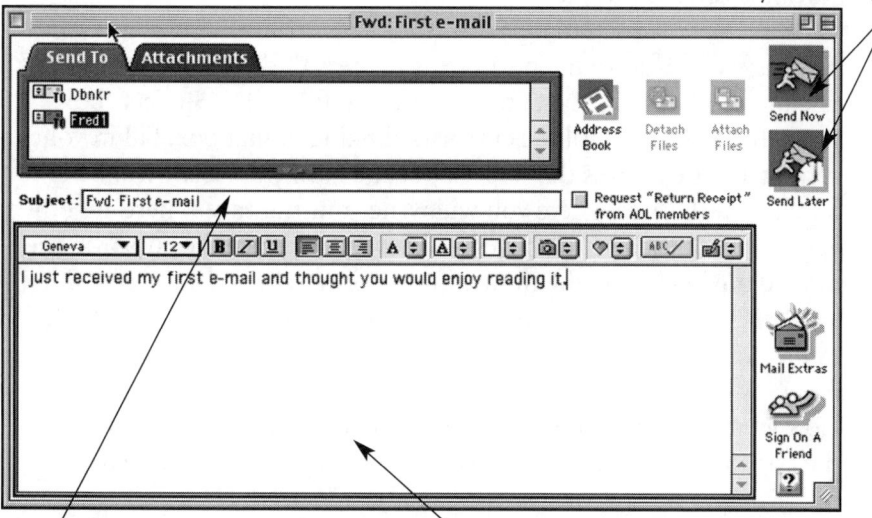

Fill in the subject of your message here or keep the original subject.

Add your message here.

57

The First Week with My New iMac

Yes, but how do I forward this message (or any message) to my daughter when her address is not already in the "Send To" box?

Good question. The cursor will be blinking in the "Send To" box. Point the cursor on your address book just to the right of this box and open it by pressing on the mouse button once (clicking). If you are lucky, the nice person who helped you set up the computer also filled in the e-mail addresses of family and friends. If not, you need to look in Chapter 11; where this procedure is explained in detail.

Look for the name of the person to whom you wish to forward the message. (If you have lots of names, use the arrow key to scroll down the list.) Highlight the name of the correct person and then point the cursor on the name and press the mouse button twice (double-click).

Look at the "Send To" box. The correct e-mail address is now there. If you want to send the message to more that one person, just do the same thing again and another e-mail address will be added to this box. When you have added all the addresses to whom you wish to send this message, close this window by pointing the mouse cursor on the small square on the upper left side of the window (the "Close" box) and pressing the mouse button once (clicking).

Now it is time to learn another "trick"!

The easy way to go to the next box is to press the "tab" key. You have filled in the "Send To" box and you want to fill in the "Subject" box. Press the "tab" key until the cursor is blinking in that box. Fill in your subject and then press the "tab" key again. Now the cursor will be blinking in the area where you will write your message. There are other ways to get to each of the boxes—one way is to place the cursor in the desired box and press the mouse button once (click). *However, using the "tab" key to move around is a very important skill and something that you need to remember.*

Now let me make another point. You do not have to do anything with the e-mail that you have been sent. No one says that you have to

The Time Has Come

answer it. You may want to read it, you may not. You may want to wait to read it at another time, and that is fine. Nothing is going to happen to the mail you have been sent. It does not get lost. It actually goes to a "Mail Center" and it is kept in a file called "Incoming/Saved Mail." If you do choose to wait to read it or you wish to reply to it later, it will be there for you for several days.

You can now get your next message. Look at the arrows on the upper right of the message box and, with the cursor on the left or right arrow, press the mouse button once (click). Your next piece of e-mail will appear. When you close that message (do this by pointing the cursor on the "square" in the upper left corner and clicking), you will see the "New Mail" list once again. By highlighting another line with the arrow keys and pressing the "return" key (or using the mouse), you can now read another e-mail message.

Let me be the first to warn you that you may not want to open and read all the e-mail that is sent to you. Often there will be mail from unknown people or groups that offer sexually explicit photos or fantastic opportunities to buy things. The general rule is that if you do not recognize the user name, do not open the e-mail. This might be difficult for you in the beginning because you are unfamiliar with all the "addresses" of family and friends. You can keep a list near the computer as a reference. Or you can just recognize that in the first few weeks you might wind up opening some mail with unexpected results!

If you want to get rid of unwanted e-mail, the way to do this is to "delete" the message. This is very easy to do. Look at the list of your incoming e-mail and see if you wish to get rid of messages from unknown sources, or old messages that are no longer of interest. Notice that under the message box there are several gray rectangular "buttons"; on the left there is one labeled "Delete." Point the cursor on this button and press the mouse button once (click). You will see a message after you press the "Delete" button that asks you if you really want to delete this message. (This is a safeguard to give you a chance to reverse your decision.) Point the cursor on either the "Delete" or the "Cancel" button and click. Another way to do this is to press the "esc" key on the

59

keyboard to cancel or press the "return" key to delete. The message is now gone. (If you wish to delete a message that you have already opened, just follow the same procedure.)

Setting Up an ISP Account

If no one has helped you to set up an account, go to the right side of your desktop. There you will see several icons. Point the cursor on the one that looks like a gray rectangle and says "Macintosh HD." Press the mouse button twice (double-click) to open it. Then point the mouse cursor on the folder that says "Internet" and again press the mouse button twice (double-click). The iMac comes with three Internet Service Provider applications that are preinstalled. They are "Microsoft Internet Explorer," "Netscape Communicator," and "America Online" which is the ISP that I am describing. Go to the AOL icon and press the mouse button twice (double-click). Follow the instructions for setting up an account. Or you can put the America Online CD into the CD drive and follow the installation instructions for a free trial period of 250 (or more) hours. This is plenty of time to learn how to do a variety of tasks. Then you can choose which ISP you would like to use.

Your E-mail Address

Your e-mail address consists of two parts. The first is your user name, which you get to choose. The second part tells everyone which ISP you are using. YOU MUST GIVE PEOPLE YOUR WHOLE E-MAIL ADDRESS. It is like the street, city, state, and zip code that you use to receive regular mail (cutely referred to as "snail mail" by the computer crowd). To just say, "my address is PLF" or "my address is .com" is the equivalent of giving your home address as "Paul" or "803…" Your letters and magazines would never arrive at your house, and the same is true for e-mail.

Here's another important piece of advice. If you have a friend or acquaintance with whom you rarely speak (you know the one—the person you don't want to have much to do with, but you were raised to be polite so you get together every few months for lunch), and he or she asks you if you have an e-mail address, your answer is *NO!* You *do*

The Time Has Come

not have to be polite about *everything*! If you do not want to talk on the telephone with this person, why would you want to receive "mail" every day from him or her? If you really are that polite, you will feel the need to write back. Now you have a "relationship" with someone you don't even want to see regularly.

Chapter 7
More to the Internet than Just E-mail: The World Wide Web Is Waiting!

I told you there were other things to notice on the America Online (AOL) "Welcome" window (see figure 7.1). The first important item is on the far right of the window and says "My Weather." The current temperature for your area is sometimes shown just underneath the heading. Better yet, what is really great is that if you point the cursor on the words "My Weather" and press the mouse button once (click), a new window appears with both current and future forecasts. This is even better than the Weather Channel!

The First Week with My New iMac

In the same "Welcome" window you will sometimes see the name of the city or town where you live. (It is usually at the bottom of the window near the middle, or it is titled "Local" in a vertical list on the left side of the window, along with a list of other interesting things.) If you point the cursor on Local and press the mouse button once (click), a new window will appear with all sorts of information telling you what is happening around your town. Aside from special events and news, you can usually get current movie listings. This is a lot easier than going to the newspaper.

Figure 7.1

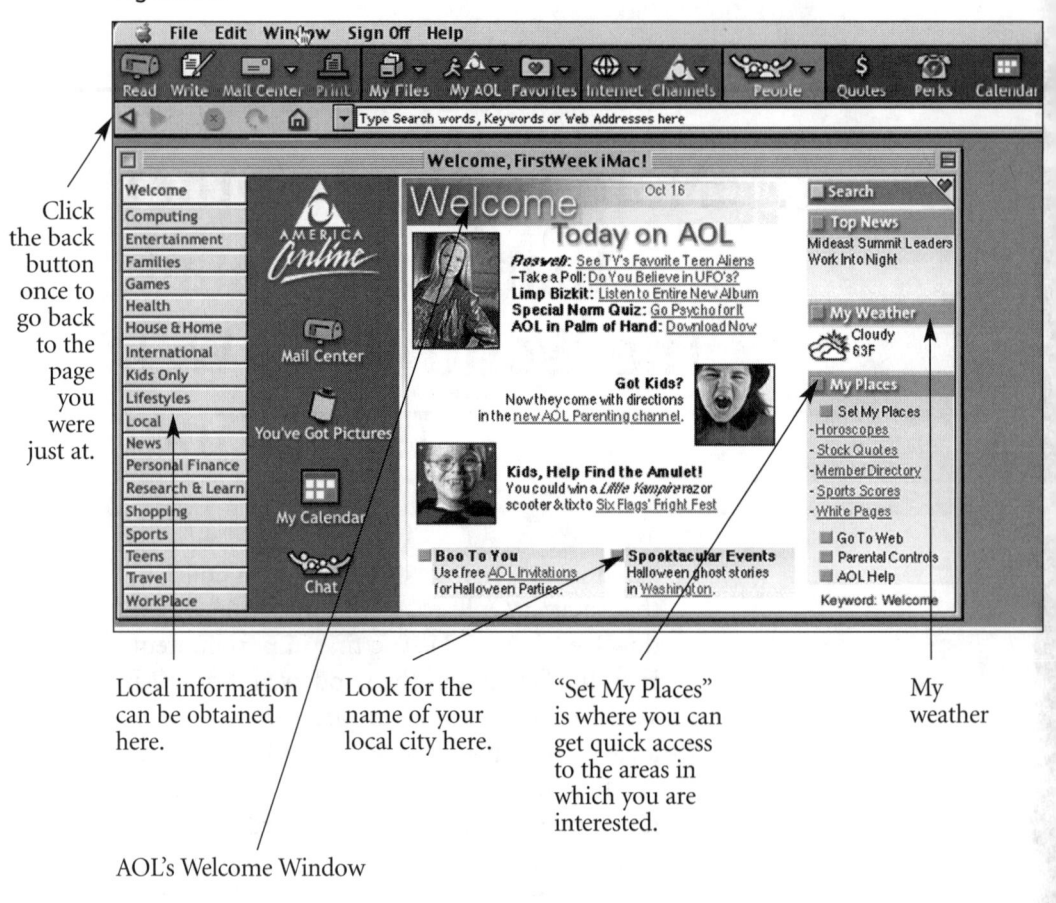

Click the back button once to go back to the page you were just at.

Local information can be obtained here.

Look for the name of your local city here.

"Set My Places" is where you can get quick access to the areas in which you are interested.

My weather

AOL's Welcome Window

More to the Internet than Just E-Mail

When you have some time, you might want to try pointing the cursor on any of the items on the left side of this window and clicking on the mouse button. Take the time to look over the different bits of information in each area. It is good practice, and you might find a favorite item or area. Remember, if you do not want to see a particular window, go to the backward arrow on the left side of the toolbar. For each left click you will go back one page.

Those Dedicated to Watching the Stock Market—This Is Your Section
(Non-Portfolio Watchers, Skip This Section and Go to "Surfing The Web")

Something else to notice on the AOL "Welcome" window is a heading on the lower right side called "My Places." Just under that heading is a box with the heading "Set My Places." If you point the cursor on this box and press the mouse button (click), you are given a new window and offered five settings (see figure 7.2). Make the first one "My Portfolios" from the "Personal Finance" category. This is your entrance to the stock market. Just point the cursor on this title, click, and you are connected to the latest Wall Street information. You can even customize the screen by adding a folder of your own investments. Then, every time you click on "My Portfolios" and open to the name of a particular portfolio, a listing of all your positions will appear along with their current price and other information (see figure 7.3).

You might want to have your most recent brokerage statement next to you to make it easier to "fill in all the blanks." After pointing the cursor on "My Portfolios," press the mouse button once (click). A new window will appear and you will see the words "My Portfolios" in black letters on a multicolored background (see figure 7.3). For instant stock quotations you can just point the cursor below this where it says "Quotes" and click. Then fill in the symbol (letters that identify each company) in the appropriate space. Another way you can get current stock quotations is by going directly to the icon bar at the top of the window and finding the fourth icon from the right, which shows a "$"

The First Week with My New iMac

over the word "Quotes." Point the cursor at this icon and press the mouse button once (click) to get individual stock prices and information.

Figures 7.2 and 7.3

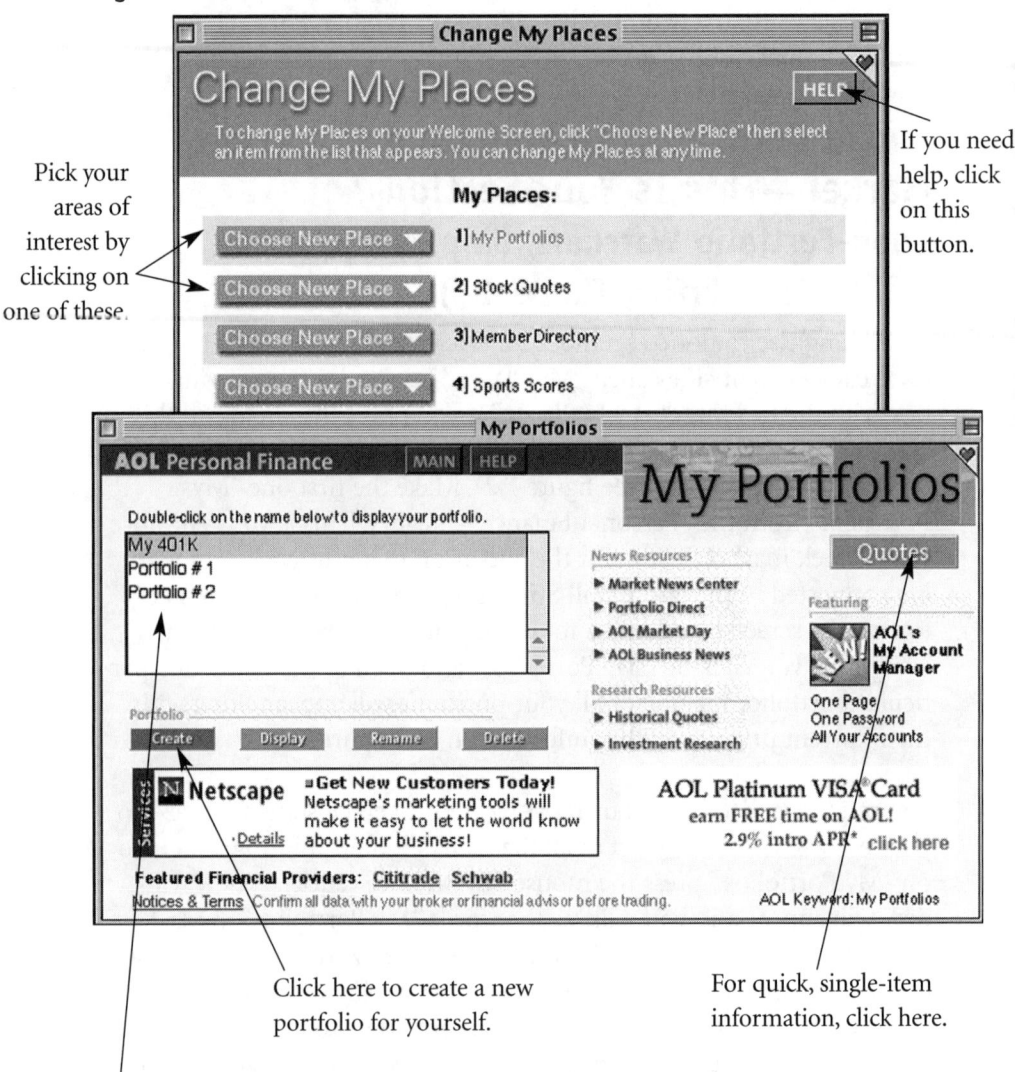

Pick your areas of interest by clicking on one of these.

If you need help, click on this button.

Change My Places

To change My Places on your Welcome Screen, click "Choose New Place" then select an item from the list that appears. You can change My Places at any time.

My Places:

Choose New Place ▼ 1] My Portfolios
Choose New Place ▼ 2] Stock Quotes
Choose New Place ▼ 3] Member Directory
Choose New Place ▼ 4] Sports Scores

My Portfolios

AOL Personal Finance MAIN HELP

Double-click on the name below to display your portfolio.

My 401K
Portfolio # 1
Portfolio # 2

Portfolio
Create Display Rename Delete

News Resources
► Market News Center
► Portfolio Direct
► AOL Market Day
► AOL Business News

Research Resources
► Historical Quotes
► Investment Research

Quotes

Featuring
AOL's My Account Manager
One Page
One Password
All Your Accounts

Netscape — "Get New Customers Today! Netscape's marketing tools will make it easy to let the world know about your business!
·Details

AOL Platinum VISA Card
earn FREE time on AOL!
2.9% intro APR* click here

Featured Financial Providers: Cititrade Schwab
Notices & Terms Confirm all data with your broker or financial advisor before trading.
AOL Keyword: My Portfolios

Click here to create a new portfolio for yourself.

For quick, single-item information, click here.

You will see the name of each portfolio here.

More to the Internet than Just E-Mail

"My Portfolios" window has a large box within which you can place the names of all the different portfolios you wish to create. (Let me mention that you may also just want one of your children to put all your financial information on the computer for you. They may think that it is easier to use another program like Quicken® to manage and record your financial information. However, there is no reason that you cannot do this all yourself; it is really not that difficult—and after all, this is why you bought this guide. I personally think it is a lot of fun to "check in" once a day or so and see what is happening "on the Street.")

So assuming that you wish to continue, look in the lower left corner of the window. You will see four colored rectangles with white letters (see figure 7.3). The first one from the left says "Create." Point the cursor on this box and press the mouse button once (click). A new window will appear that says "Step 1: New Portfolio Setup" on the title bar. The cursor will be blinking in the box in which you need to type a name for your portfolio. All you have to do is think of a name you wish to use. An example would be to use your initials, the name of the brokerage house where this account is held, or simply "mine." Then press the "return" key or click on the "Next" button.

Now we get to the difficult part. Look at this next window ("Step 2"). This one requires a lot of information. That is why it would be helpful to have your most recent brokerage statement in front of you (see figure 7.4).

Go ahead and type in the necessary information in each of the appropriate boxes. Remember: The easiest way to move from box to box is to press the "tab" key *lightly*! (The alternative is to place the cursor in each box and click the mouse button once.) You may also add "cash" to your portfolio, but you need to do that as a separate addition, as the computer will warn you! When you have put in as much information as you wish (you do not have to fill in every box), point the cursor on the "Add Item" button to the right and press the mouse button once (click).

The First Week with My New iMac

Figure 7.4

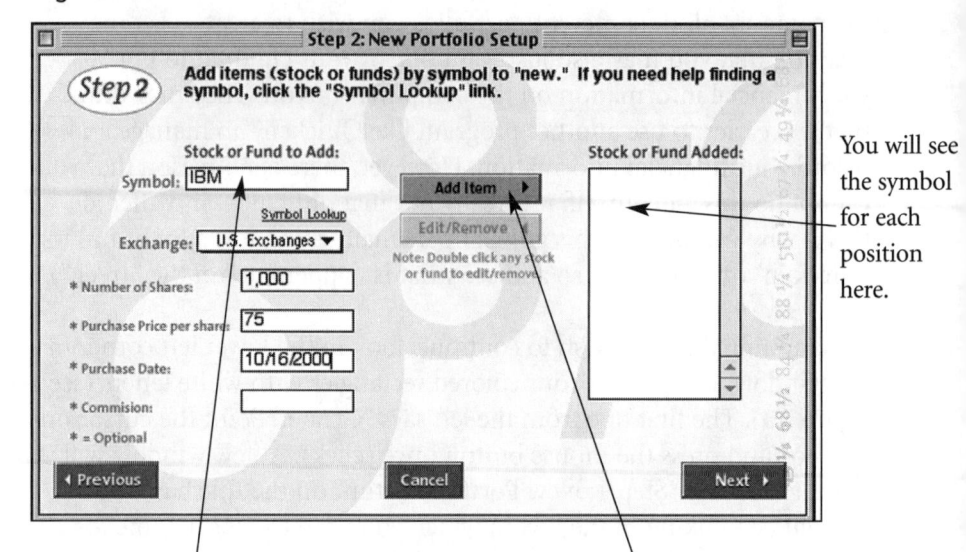

```
┌─────────────── Step 2: New Portfolio Setup ───────────────┐
│  ┌─────┐   Add items (stock or funds) by symbol to "new." If you need help finding a│
│  │Step2│   symbol, click the "Symbol Lookup" link.         │
│  └─────┘                                                    │
│                                                             │
│         Stock or Fund to Add:           Stock or Fund Added:│
│      Symbol: │IBM  │                                        │
│                    Symbol Lookup    ┌─ Add Item  ▶ ─┐       │
│    Exchange: │U.S. Exchanges ▼│     ┌─ Edit/Remove ─┐       │
│                                     Note: Double click any stock│
│  * Number of Shares: │1,000│        or fund to edit/remove  │
│                                                             │
│  * Purchase Price per share: │75│                           │
│                                                             │
│  * Purchase Date: │10/16/2000│                              │
│                                                             │
│  * Commission:     │     │                                  │
│  * = Optional                                               │
│                                                             │
│  ◀ Previous │         │ Cancel │         │ Next ▶ │         │
└─────────────────────────────────────────────────────────────┘
```

You will see
the symbol
for each
position
here.

Type in the symbol for   After filling in the information about your stock,
  your position here.   click on this button to add it to your portfolio.

On the right side you will see that this particular position has been added to your portfolio. Repeat this process for each position that you want to add. If you make a mistake, just highlight the item that you do not want (when it is highlighted it will be visible as a colored bar) and click on the button below "Add Item" that says "Edit/Remove." You can now make changes or remove this item from your portfolio.

Now point the cursor on the "Next" button and press the mouse button once to move to the next window ("Step 3"), which allows you to add cash and use indices. Congratulations! You have now started to create a working portfolio all by yourself. Point the mouse cursor at the "Finish" button and press the mouse button once (click). The final window will tell you some of the things you will be able to do with your new portfolio.

When you click "OK," the next thing you will see is that your portfolio will open and the positions you just added are now displayed. The information in front of you will tell you the symbol of your position,

More to the Internet than Just E-Mail

the current/closing price, the change, your gains/losses based on your purchase price information, and the current value of this position. Look at the bottom of the window, which gives you lots of other options to choose from, go ahead and click on whatever interests you. Have fun!

Surfing the Web

Now it is time to start "surfing the Web." This can be a lot of fun or totally frustrating. It is fun to see all the companies, organizations, and government agencies that can give you interesting information. You can learn about new products, get the exhibition schedule for your local museum, see what stories will be presented on the television show *60 Minutes*, read a magazine or newspaper and get the local movie schedule, etc., etc. You can even connect with the Web page of a foreign city and plan details of a future trip. These are the fun parts.

The frustrating part is that sometimes you are given too much information. It is difficult to sort through everything to get to the special item that interests you. Sorry, that is just the way it is right now. Once you have found a particular home page that you like or need you can "mark" it by making it one of your "Favorites" so that you can get back to it quickly. However, getting to that in the first place takes thought and patience.

AOL version 5.0 makes this a little easier for you, because it allows you to pick five areas called "My Places." Look at the lower right side of the AOL "Welcome" window (see figures 7.1 and 7.2). Under "My Places" is a box with "Set My Places." Point the cursor on this box and press the mouse button once (click). You now have a great number of areas that might interest you. Within each area there are subheadings to narrow down your choices. Follow the prompts to pick five areas that you want to "get to" quickly. These will then be available immediately every time you log on. All you have to do is click on them.

So back to actually searching for something in particular. The best is to just jump in and try it out. Notice that above the large AOL window in the middle of your desktop there are several bars. The first is a menu bar

The First Week with My New iMac

(a gray line with the title of each menu) and then just below it is a line with multicolored rectangles. Under that line is another gray line. In the middle of this third line is a box that says "Type Search words, Keywords or Web Addresses here" and to the right there is a button that says "GO." Point the cursor in this box, press the mouse button *once* to *highlight* the current words in the box. Then type in a word—the "keyword"—that describes whatever it is that interests you. Or type in a Web address that you have gotten from an article, an advertisement, or from television. (You can tell it is a Web address as it will begin "www." followed by the name of the company, group, or institution and then completed with the famous ".com" or ".org" etc.; see figure 7.5).

Figure 7.5 — Menu Bar

This is how you can easily get on the Internet. Type in your web address or keyword and click on "Go" or press the return key.

Or, you can click here "Go To Web" and a window will pop up that allows you to type in a Web site address.

Now this is just practice. You do not need to agonize over what to type. Pick anything! If you want a suggestion, try typing in www.nbc.com and then press the "return" key. This will connect you to the Web page of this television company. Look around its "home page" and see all the different kinds of information it offers. When you point the cursor on something that interests you a hand will appear. (See more on this below.) This means that you can press the mouse button (click) here

More to the Internet than Just E-Mail

and learn more about that item. Another idea is to type in the word "gastrointestinal." Wait until you see the possibilities of that keyword! (**Note:** The on-line bookseller Barnes & Noble, www.bn.com, is ready to offer you lots of books on this subject if you click on its "link" on the side of the window.) My mother wanted to look at the Web page for the Metropolitan Opera in New York City so she typed in www.metopera.org. Now she knows everything about the upcoming season. One of my favorites is www.bluemountain.com, a source of free electronic greeting cards. Not only does it have cards for *every* occasion, not only will it send as many "electronic" cards as you like to as many people as you like for free, but it also can send greeting cards in a dozen different languages!

After you have typed in something, wait a moment and you will see a page that offers you all sorts of information pertaining to the organization or group. You can place your cursor on whatever you like and press the mouse button once (click). If you wait, another page will appear giving you the information you asked for and offering you "links" to additional information or offering other choices.

Please note the following:

- If something is written in blue and underlined, this is a "link," and pointing the cursor on it and pressing the mouse button once will take you straight to that information.

- If you want to see the previous page, go to the "back" arrow at the extreme left of the lowest gray line.

- After you have gone back a page or two, you can go forward again by clicking on the "forward" arrow just to the right of the "back" arrow. (Think of the arrows as similar to those on the controls of your VCR—another piece of electronic equipment that might frustrate you!)

- Look at all the items at the top and bottom of most Web pages, as they really help guide you around the "site" and also help get you back to the beginning or "home page."

The First Week with My New iMac

- You do not need to know the address of a Web site. You can experiment and see if you get what you want. How? Type in "www." followed by the name you think your group would use, followed by ".com" if it is commercial, ".edu" if it is an educational institution, or ".org" if it is a non-profit. Then press "return." If it works, great! If not, try to think of another name that the group would use and try again. This is also the time to try a "keyword." Fill in the word or words that describe what you want to know about or need. Then press the "return" key. Look over the list that is provided in your category and select whatever looks best. (You can always "go back" to the original list and try another choice.)

- Another way to try and find something is to use what is called a "search engine." Examples are www.yahoo.com, www.lycos.com, www.snap.com, www.northernlight.com, www.askjeeves.com, and www.altavista.com. These are sites that are specifically designed to find information for you— information that is written in a more complete and easily understood format. With more than a *billion* Web sites, it is impossible for any of these "engines" to search all but a relatively small percentage of the Web. However, new search engines are appearing every week. It is well worth trying each of these to see which ones work best for you.

- When you get tired of all this just *shut it down.* How? By pointing the cursor on the box in the top left corner of the Web page (the "Close" box) and pressing the mouse button once (clicking). Now you can play one of the nice card games or just go read a book!

- There is obviously more to learn about the "Web," but this is a start.

- For a number of Web site addresses that I think might be of interest to you, please check Appendix C.

Chapter 8

Some Simple Basic Fun??? This Is Like the Piano! Do I Really Have to Practice One Hour a Day?

The *bad* news is that it would really be helpful if you played with the computer every day for about an hour. The *good* news is that you do not have to do "work"! One of your tasks is to play some of the games that come with your computer.

The First Week with My New iMac

If your nice young person followed the suggestions in Chapter 3, you should have an icon on the right side of your desktop that looks like a deck of cards and says "Solitaire." If not, there are several things you can do. You can get the game off of one of the CDs that came with your iMac. (The "Install CD" has a folder called "CD Extras" in which you will find "Eric's Solitaire." Drag this item to your desktop for easy access.) Another way to get a game is that you can practice "downloading" a game from the Internet by going on-line, typing in the address www.cnet.com/games, and clicking on the type of game you wish to play. The best idea is to get a CD from the computer store with a whole lot of games on it that you will enjoy besides solitaire. Then you can load your own games into the computer. In any case let's assume you do have the card game solitaire and start with that one.

You know the drill by now—point the cursor on the solitaire icon and press the mouse button twice (double-click). The cards are waiting in front of you. If you do not know how to play the game, DO NOT go to the "Help" menu. In "Eric's Solitaire" you need to go to the "Options" menu to find help. (Remember, the easy way is to put the cursor on "Options" and press the mouse button once [click].) You can always use the shortcut or quick way to get help, which is to use the keyboard command. Press the "Command" key plus the "H" key simultaneously (⌘+H). Help "Topics" will give you a number of hints about playing the game.

If you do know how to play the game, terrific. However, you are probably wondering how to move the cards. Do you remember that I told you that you would need to know how to "click and drag"? Well, this is where you can practice!

Place the cursor on the card that you wish to move. *Hold down* the mouse button. *While holding down the mouse button,* move the mouse over to the card on which you wish to place your card. Then release the mouse button.

If the card moved to the right spot, congratulations! You are a natural. However, it is just as likely that the card popped back into its original

Some Simple Basic Fun???

column. What might have happened is that you released the mouse button too soon. Do not worry. That is just fine. In fact that is great, because this is the reason you are playing a card game. You do not have to tell anyone that you are playing solitaire. Instead, tell them that you are practicing "clicking and dragging"!

Having said that, go ahead and try to move the card again. Keep doing this and, as you get better, you will see that you do not have to grip the mouse quite so tightly. (In addition, you will learn that you do not have to twist your hand/arm/shoulder to get the cursor to the right spot! Remember, "body English" does not help in any sport—even computer games! Also, when you are about to go off the mouse pad, lift up the mouse and place it back in the middle of the mouse pad.)

If you have no move, it is time to go to the deck of cards in the lower left corner of the game board. Place the cursor on the deck and press the mouse button once (click). The third card is turned over. Do this

The First Week with My New iMac

again and the next "third" card is revealed. If you can use any of these cards, you need to place the cursor on the card, press the mouse button and, *while holding down the mouse button,* move the card where it should go. Then release the mouse button. (Figure 8.1 portrays a game of solitaire.)

When you have come to the last card, you will see a small multicolored square to show you that you have run through the whole deck. If you want to go through the deck again, just point the cursor on the square and press the mouse button once (click). The whole thing starts over again. You can change some of the aspects of the game by pointing the cursor on the "Options" menu and pressing the mouse button once (clicking) to bring down the menu. Point the cursor on "Preferences," press the mouse button once, then make the choices you want. Be sure to point the cursor on "OK" and click so the computer makes the changes.

When you have given up on the game you have been dealt, or when you are ready to play a new hand, go to the "File" menu and click on "New Game." (The keyboard command for this is to press the "Command" key (⌘) and the "N" key simultaneously.) Now you are ready to start over.

Figure 8.1

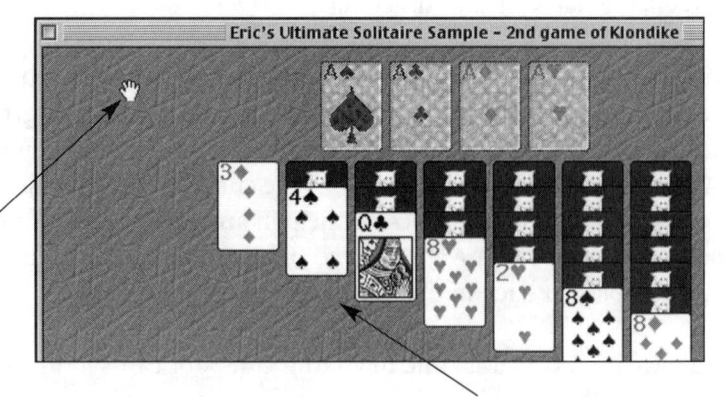

In this game, the cursor will look like a hand.

This is the game board of Eric's solitaire with cards in midgame.

76

Some Simple Basic Fun???

By purchasing your own game CD, there will be several other card games that you might enjoy playing. Notice that each one has a different technique for moving the cards. Either read the directions or just go ahead and try different things. You might find it unsettling to have the format and computer instructions change from one game to the next. Please understand that each game or program is created by a different group of people. They do things the way that they think works best. This is just something that you have to live with. What is intuitive for them will probably be foreign to you in the beginning. Keep at it. I promise it will soon be comfortable.

A personal note: I can tell you from experience that the computer does not deal easy games. I have spent most of the night trying to "beat" the machine. I was visiting my mother to help her with her new computer, but she could not practice her new skills because I was determined to continue playing solitaire until I won!

Chapter 9
Writing Documents and Correspondence: I Am Already in the Middle of the Book and I Still Don't Know How to Write a Letter!

> I am sympathetic with your frustration, but if this is the most important task on your list I am sure that you have skipped ahead to this chapter!

The First Week with My New iMac

Explaining how to produce and save documents and correspondence is probably the most difficult section of this book. It is difficult because you can use several programs to do the same tasks. It is difficult because each program works in a slightly different way. It is difficult because each of these writing programs offers more choices, more icons, more menu bars, and more ways for things to go wrong than any other program you will use. Finally, it is most difficult because many of us are still trying to learn what half of these things do ourselves!

Once again, rather than discussing all the different programs available, I will explain how to do some basic tasks using a program with which I am familiar and that I feel is very "user friendly." That program is AppleWorks® and it comes with the iMac as one of the applications. This is not to say that one program is better than another. In fact I think several companies make excellent applications that can be used on the iMac. (Some popular examples are Microsoft Word® and Corel WordPerfect®, which are very easy to use.) I pick just one program to explain because I would like this book and these instructions to be slightly shorter than the Manhattan telephone directory!

Whichever program you choose to use as your primary document writing program, the most important thing to remember is to *save all your work* and do it as you are going along. *Everyone* is told this and *no one* bothers to do it. That is, they do not bother to "save as they go along" until a very important paper or letter is suddenly lost after they have spent half a day working on it! Another possibility is that a drink spills on your machine, a virus/worm gets in and wipes out all your memory, or someone walks off with your laptop. One experience like this and one learns to "save" every 5 to 10 minutes. (While writing this book, I was pressing the "Command" key and the "S" key to save things after almost every paragraph. Whenever I stopped to think about the next phrase, or whenever I made a correction, it was my natural reflex.) There's more on "saving your work" later in this chapter, but let me mention that much depends on which word-processing program you are using. Some word-processing programs are designed to save automatically. AppleWorks does not.

80

Writing Documents and Correspondence

Now Can I Write a Letter to My Cousin in England?

Assuming that you wish to use AppleWorks, we are now ready to start. You will first need to make this program the "active" window on your desktop. If your helpful young person has done as asked, you should have an icon on the right side of the desktop that looks like a folder with writing tools in a square. Under this it says "AppleWorks 5 alias." If this is so, point the cursor on this icon and press the mouse button twice (double-click).

If the icon is *not* on the desktop, do the following:

1. Point the mouse cursor on the gray rectangle that has Macintosh HD written under it. Press the mouse button twice (double-click).

2. Use the arrow key to highlight "Applications" (or point the mouse cursor on the "Applications" folder) and press the mouse button twice (double-click).

3. Use the arrow keys to highlight the folder "AppleWorks 5" (or point the mouse cursor on this folder) and press the mouse button twice (double-click). (See figure 9.1.)

4. Use the arrow keys to highlight the square "AppleWorks " (or point the mouse cursor on this folder) and press the mouse button twice (double-click).

5. *Finally,* you will see the window that lets you create a document! (Now do you see why I suggest having an "alias" [or shortcut] of this application on the desktop? See Chapter 11 for instructions on how to create an alias.)

6. Decide what you want to do (in this case we are writing a letter on a plain piece of paper so you want "Word Processing" highlighted) and press the "return" key (or click on "OK").

81

The First Week with My New iMac

Note: If all you need is a plain piece of paper, there is diamond shape in the "Applications" folder that looks like a piece of paper with a pencil writing on it and has the words "Simple Text" under it. Point the mouse cursor on this icon and press the mouse button twice (double-click). A window will appear on which you can write anything that you would like. There are no icons with this basic program so you will need to use the simple menus to change settings like fonts, including their size and style. It is really a very basic program, and I think you will not use it much unless you just need to print out a quick note or reminder for yourself.

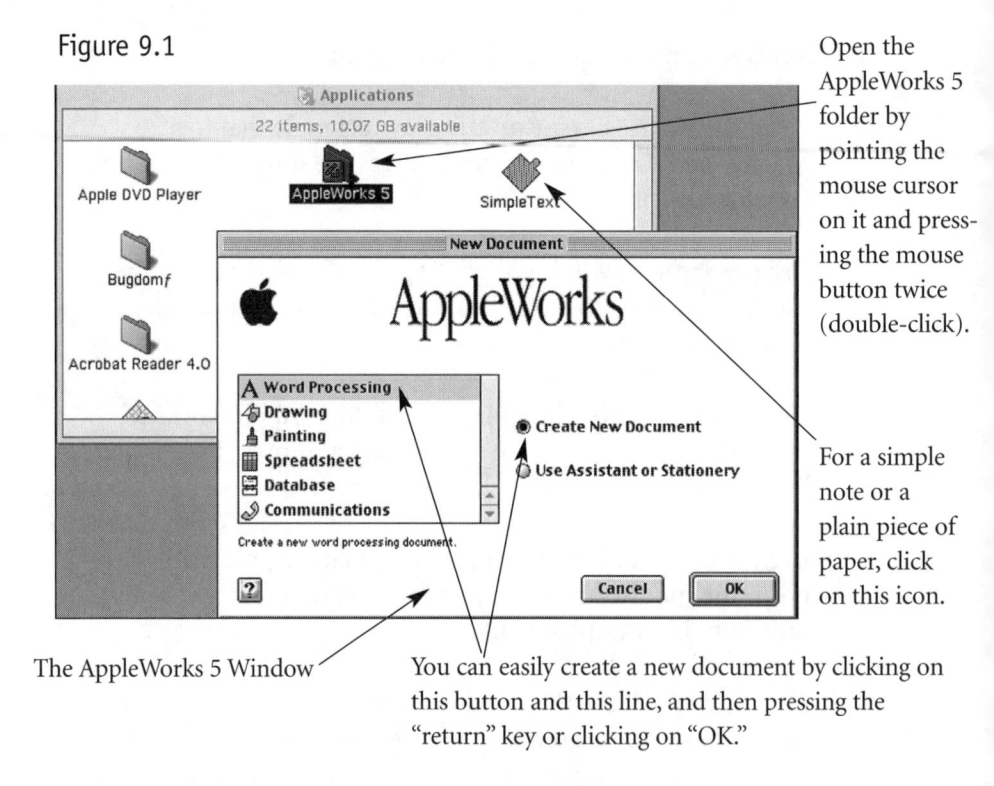

Figure 9.1

Open the AppleWorks 5 folder by pointing the mouse cursor on it and pressing the mouse button twice (double-click).

For a simple note or a plain piece of paper, click on this icon.

The AppleWorks 5 Window

You can easily create a new document by clicking on this button and this line, and then pressing the "return" key or clicking on "OK."

Now you should be looking at a large window with the words "untitled (WP)" on the title bar (see figure 9.2). The cursor will be blinking in the large open area that looks like a piece of paper. You are now ready to write anything you want. Just start typing!

Writing Documents and Correspondence

So if it was this easy, why didn't I tell you all this sooner? Well, the reason for waiting is that if you look just above the title bar you will see three rows of words and icons. At this point in the book, you are probably starting to feel comfortable with a menu bar. All that has been added to this one are some tools that you may or may not want to use when you write. The other bars are also types of "toolbars." They are usually called the "button bar" and the "format bar." In addition, there are two bars under the title bar. One is obviously a ruler that can help you arrange your margins, tabs, etc. The other has icons to help you format your document. (More on this later.)

Another thing to understand is that most of the icons you see on these two bars are also items that you will find if you press the mouse button (click) on any of the words on the menu bar. These are just quicker ways to do certain things. (They are quicker if you like using the mouse. Otherwise, you will find it helpful to have the menu bar to use keystrokes to give different commands or to see the actual words that describe what it is you want to do.)

If you have something specific that you want to write immediately, please go ahead and start typing. When you are done with the letter or list, point the cursor on the icon that looks like a printer on the button bar (the

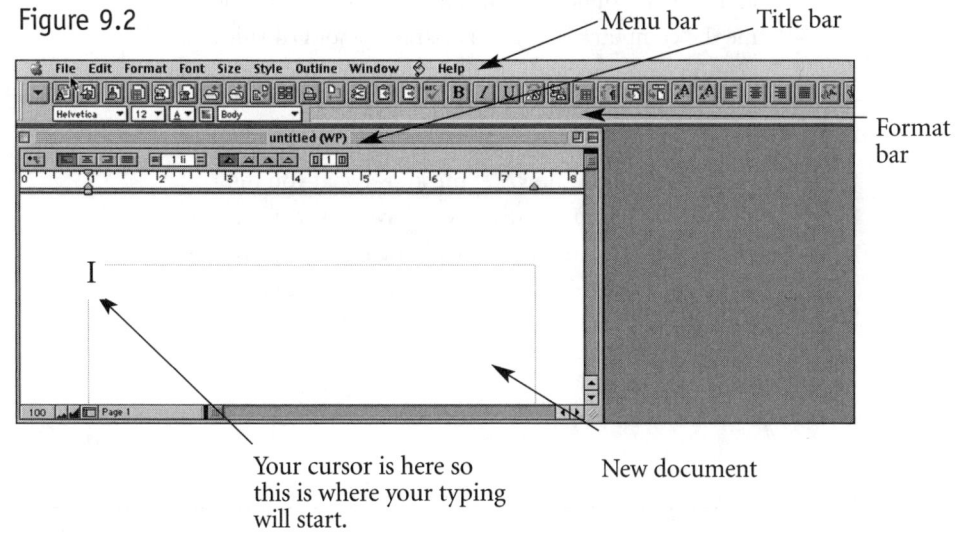

Figure 9.2

Menu bar · Title bar · Format bar · Your cursor is here so this is where your typing will start. · New document

83

The First Week with My New iMac

Dear Doris,

I am happy to hear that all is well and that you had a lovely holiday in the country. I can imagine that the garden must look wonderful after all the rain you had last month. I hope that your visitors from Switzerland appreciated all the work and preparation that went into this.

Everything is fine here. I have been totally occupied—day and night—with my newest "toy." I bought myself a COMPUTER! I know you will think I am crazy, but I really wanted to communicate with Beth and Paul on a regular basis, and they tell me that the best way to do this is to "e-mail" them. I also want to be able to make corrections easily when typing a letter rather than redoing everything several times because I forgot a line. In addition, you would not believe the fun I am having looking up things on the "World Wide Web"!

Then my friend Silvia told me about some wonderful games that I can play on the computer. I am sometimes up late at night unable to stop until I "beat" the computer. I know it sounds silly, but my orthopedic surgeon told me the computer is as good as knitting for arthritis prevention, and I really think that the games are helping me keep my fingers and hands more flexible.

Well, that is all for now. Let me know what you think of all this. More importantly, if you have an e-mail address, please send it to me. Think of all the money we will save on postage and telephone calls if we use the Internet!

Love,

Writing Documents and Correspondence

second line, 11th item, under the "O" in the word "Outline") and press the mouse button twice (double-click). Then skip ahead to page 93 to the section on saving your work. You can come back to this next part whenever you want to learn how to do more with this program.

For those who are not in a hurry, it is time to experiment. This is not an important letter or your holiday shopping list, so it does not matter if you wipe out whole paragraphs or recopy the same line five times. This is just a fun way to learn.

Let's start at the beginning. In front of you is something that looks like a white piece of paper. The first thing we will do is pretend to write a letter to Cousin Doris in London. Go ahead and write a letter the way you would on any typewriter. If you like, you can copy my letter so that we can work on the formatting together step by step.

Now, if you are like me, you made lots of little typing errors while writing your letter or copying mine. (Again, if you just copy my letter, it might make it easier to follow some of the things I tell you to do.)

Spell Check—Your Own Personal Editor

The first thing I would like to mention is that as you were typing you may have noticed that some of your words were misspelled. Perhaps you "backspaced" with the "delete" key when you saw an error and retyped the word. If you only spotted the mistake after you finished typing, then one way of making a correction is to point the cursor in the middle of the incorrect word and press the mouse button twice (double-click). Now the whole word is highlighted. Either start retyping the word, or press the "delete" key, to remove the word and retype it correctly.

Still another way to make a correction is to point the cursor to the right of the wrong letter(s) and press the mouse button (click). You are placing the cursor at a certain spot, the insertion point, so that you can make a change. Now you can use the "delete" key to erase the mistake and then retype the correct letters. (After you are done with your corrections, be sure to point the cursor and click at the spot where you

The First Week with My New iMac

wish to continue typing. This is the insertion point. Otherwise you may find your next paragraph in the middle of your first sentence. It is something we all do in the beginning because we forget!)

To have the computer check your work:

Keyboard Command:
Press the "Command" key and the "=" key (⌘+=) simultaneously and release. Next decide if you wish to make the changes suggested, skip that word, have the Spell Check learn that word as one of your "usuals," or cancel the operation.

Mouse Command:
Point the mouse cursor at the icon that has the letters "ABC" over a red check mark. (It's on the button bar, second line down, 16th icon from the left, just under the "Scripts" menu icon.) Press the mouse button once (click) and a window will appear with your misspelled word in the top box. Suggestions for changes are in the box below. To the right, you are given several choices that include making or ignoring the suggested change, learning the new word, or canceling Spell Check (see figures 9.3 and 9.4).

Still one more way to start Spell Check is to point the mouse cursor on the word "Edit" on the menu bar and press the mouse button once (click). Go down to the term "Writing Tools" and notice that a submenu appears when you highlight it. The submenu offers you not only a spell checker, but also a thesaurus, a word counter, and other useful tools.

Now, if you did not notice this happening, you are either an excellent speller or typist, or you should go back and look at the letter to see if there really are some misspellings that you have missed. One of the nice features of this program is that you can rush ahead typing all your thoughts and not worry about some misspelled words; when you are done you can use Spell Check to make the necessary corrections. It also helps those who do not spell very well, as it points out words that you might have assumed to be correct. (**Note:** If you don't see any misspelled words it does not mean that there are no errors. It is possible that you included a word that is spelled correctly, but is not the word

Writing Documents and Correspondence

Figure 9.3

If the correct replacement word is highlighted, just point the mouse cursor here and press the mouse button once (click) or press the "return" key.

Spell check box with a misspelled word and several choices

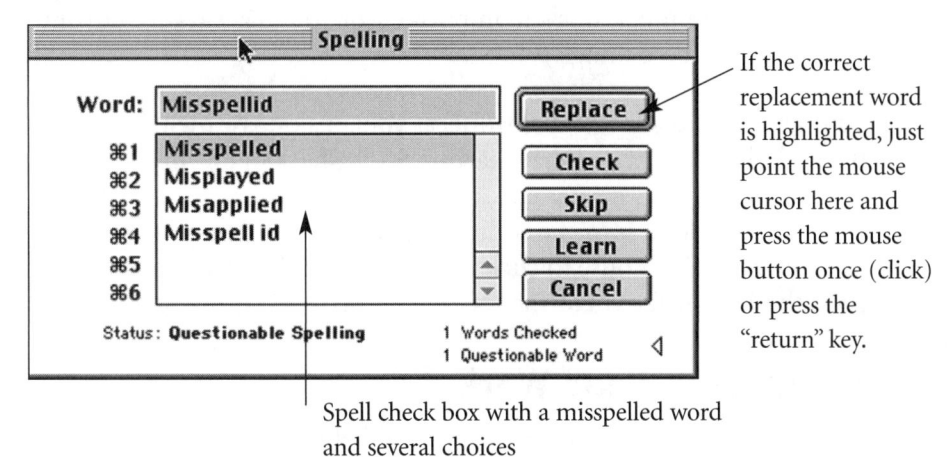

Figure 9.4

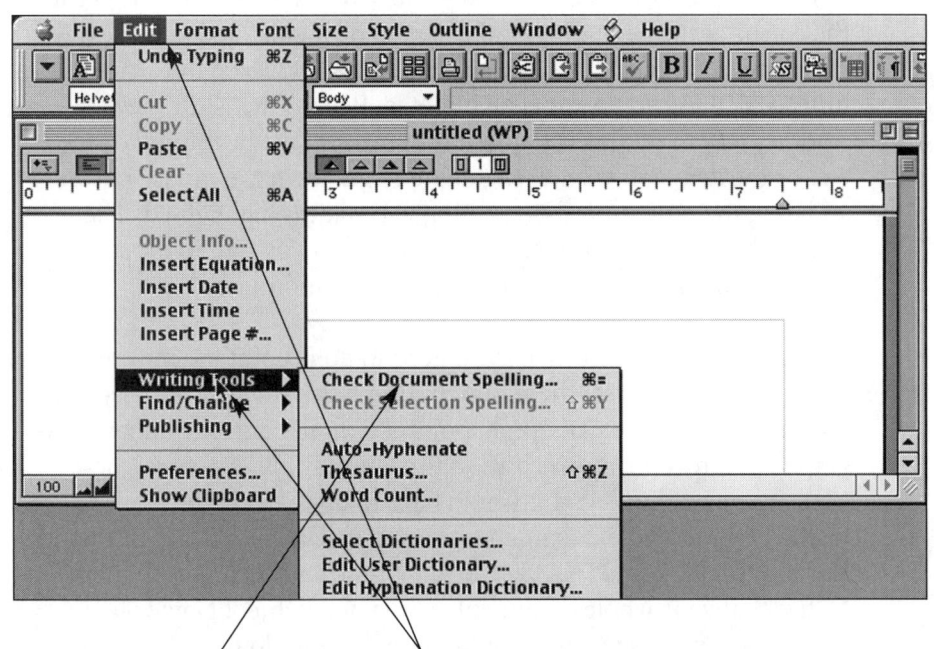

Click on "Check Document Spelling" or use the keyboard command (⌘+=).

To check your spelling, pull down the Edit Menu and highlight "Writing Tools."

The First Week with My New iMac

you meant to type. Spell Check does not consider the meaning of a word or the grammar. It is still important for you to always check your document for these things.)

You can also check individual words as you go along by highlighting the underlined word and then starting Spell Check in one of the three ways described above. After checking the highlighted word, Spell Check will ask if you want it to check the remainder of your document. You can either use the mouse to click on "Yes" or "No," or you can simply press the "Y" key for yes or the "N" key for no.

Formatting Your Work

Now, have you learned all the ways to highlight a word, phrase, or whole document? This is a very important skill. In Chapter 4 I explain how to do this using the "shift" key and arrow keys. Reminder: Point the cursor at the beginning of the area to be highlighted and press the mouse button (click). Hold down the "shift" key. Move the arrow keys until everything you want is highlighted. Release the "shift" key. Another way to do this is to place the cursor at the beginning or the end of the item you wish to highlight. Hold down the mouse button and drag the mouse until everything you want is highlighted. Then release the mouse button. Now you know why you had to practice "clicking and dragging" with the card games and tutorials!

To highlight a single word, all you need to do is point the mouse cursor on that word and press the mouse button twice *rapidly* (double-click). To highlight a whole paragraph, point the mouse cursor on that paragraph and press the mouse button three times *rapidly* (triple-click). (Bet you never thought you would have to do that!) If you want to highlight your whole document it is even easier. Press the "Command" key and the "A" key (⌘+A) at the same time and then release them. Notice that your whole document is now highlighted! Now you are probably wondering, "Why would I ever want to do that!?"

When an item is highlighted it means you have told the computer that this is something with which you want to work. What does that

Writing Documents and Correspondence

mean? Maybe you want to take out a sentence or copy a phrase and move it somewhere else. Maybe you want to change the typeface or "font" or make something bigger or smaller. Maybe you want to make that phrase **bold**, or *italicized*, or underlined. You may choose to justify (line up) something to the left or to the right, or to center it. When you highlight something, these are just some of the things you can do.

Look at the button bar and the format bar (see figure 9.5). Point the mouse at each one of the icons and see what it says in the balloons. (If you are not using balloons then look under the icons at the gray rectangle on the right side of the format bar. A description of each icon is shown there.) Some of the pictures—like the clean piece of paper or the printer—really relate to what the icons do. Others might not be so obvious. That is why it is time to experiment. Also note that most of the icons mentioned have written equivalents on the menu bar. Often you can use a key command to get the same results as clicking on an icon. As you practice, you will decide which way is best for you. For this exercise, I will use icons to perform the different tasks, but note that you can find the key commands for these tasks in Chapter 11 and Appendix B.

Figure 9.5

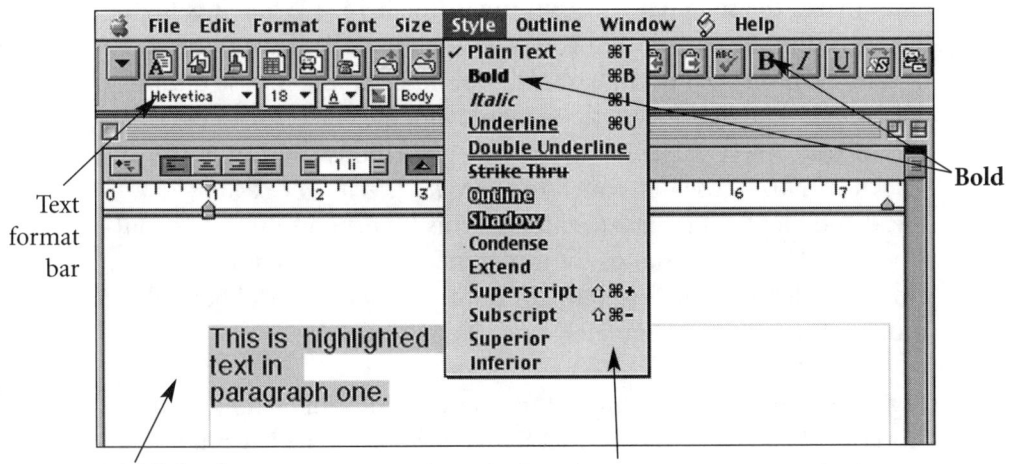

Text format bar

Highlighted text

This is the Style drop down menu. You can make the type you have highlighted bold or make other changes here.

Bold

89

The First Week with My New iMac

Go to the letter you have written. Highlight the first paragraph by pointing the cursor at the beginning of the first paragraph and pressing the mouse button once (click). Now hold down the "shift" key and move the arrow keys down and/or right until the whole paragraph is highlighted. Now release the "shift" key. (While this is the easiest, there are other ways to do this, including pointing the cursor at the start of the paragraph and then holding down the mouse button. Next drag the mouse to the right and down so that the whole paragraph is highlighted. Still another way to do this is to point the cursor in front of the first word in the first paragraph and click. Hold down the "shift" key. Point the cursor at the end of the last word in the paragraph and press the mouse button once. Release the "shift" key.)

In *my* letter everything is highlighted from "I" to "this." Now point the cursor on the "**B**" (it even looks bold) on the format bar (the second line from the top, toward the right side under "Help" on the menu bar) and press the mouse button once (click). Next "un-highlight" everything by moving the cursor anywhere on your "piece of paper" where nothing is written, and pressing once on the mouse button (clicking). Look what happened. The whole paragraph is now in **bold** face.

Go to the next paragraph and highlight the first four words. (In my letter that is the sentence, "Everything is fine here.") When it is highlighted, point the cursor on the "*I*" (notice it looks italicized) that is next to the **B** on the button bar, and press once on the mouse button (click). "Un-highlight" everything by moving the cursor to an open part of your "piece of paper" and pressing the mouse button once (clicking). Now those first four words are *italicized*. Once again, go ahead and highlight the next sentence. This time, point the mouse button on the "U," which stands for underline, and press the mouse button once (click). Then, un-highlight the sentence as you did before. Your next sentence is completely underlined.

Highlight your third paragraph. (You should really know how to do this now.) Look at the text format bar (third line on the left side). There are several white boxes with black letters and numbers. Look at the one on the left. It is telling you what font or typeface you are using right now. To change the font, point the cursor on the little down

90

Writing Documents and Correspondence

arrow to the right of the font name and press the mouse button once (click) (see figure 9.6).

A menu of different fonts will appear. You can now use the mouse to scroll down the list of possibilities. (You can actually get an idea of what most of these fonts look like because you see an example of each font in its name. However, right now that is not important; we are just playing. With practice you will find and, more importantly, remember which ones you really like. Then you can use them to make your notes more interesting.) Find the font called "Times New Roman" and when it is highlighted press the mouse button once. "Un-highlight" the third paragraph and look at the new font!

Highlight this paragraph again. Why not change the size of the font? To do this go to the box to the right, which has numbers. Point the cursor at the down arrow on the right. Press once on the mouse button and then scroll down until another size, like "18," is highlighted. Press the mouse button again and then "un-highlight" the third paragraph (see figure 9.6).

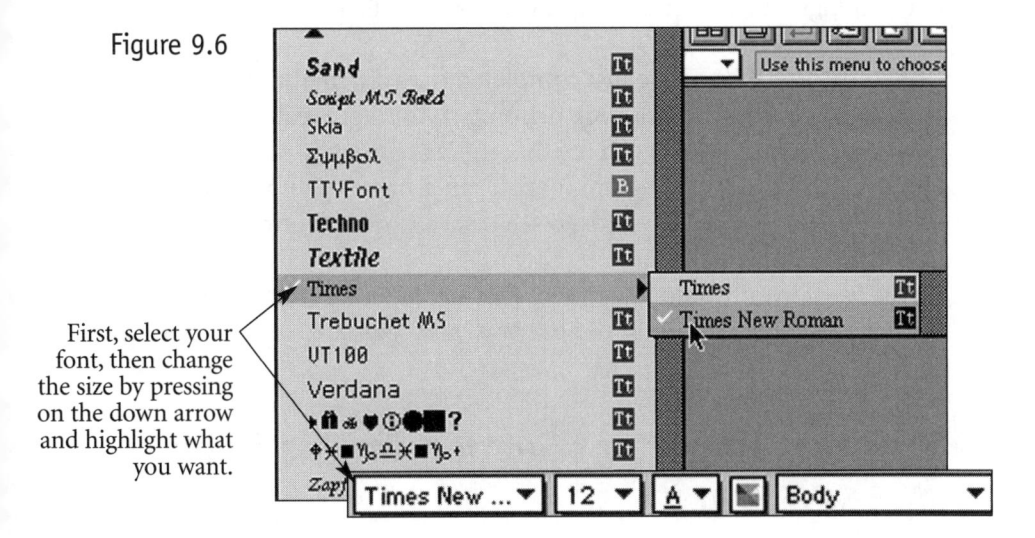

Figure 9.6

First, select your font, then change the size by pressing on the down arrow and highlight what you want.

The First Week with My New iMac

The last thing I would like you to try is "cutting and pasting." Look at the last paragraph. In my letter the first sentence is, "Well, that is all for now." Highlight that sentence and point the cursor on the icon that looks like a pair of scissors on a clipboard (button bar, second row, 11th from the right, under the "W" in Window). Press the mouse button once (click). The sentence is gone!

It is not really gone. It exists on a "clipboard" inside the computer. Point the cursor to the right of the last word in the last paragraph. **Important:** Press the mouse button so that the cursor is blinking in that spot. Point the cursor at the icon to the right of the scissors on the button bar—the one that looks like a clipboard with a forward arrow (the icon is ninth from the right). Press the mouse button once. The line you removed from the front of the paragraph is now at the end of the paragraph!

Point the cursor on the icon that looks like your printer (button bar, second row, 11th from the left, under the "O" in Outline). Press the mouse button once. Your letter is now being printed, assuming that you have turned on your printer. (The printer, like the computer, can be left on all the time. It makes things much easier, and leaving it this way will not hurt it.)

Congratulations! You have just completed *nine* different tasks or changes to your letter, including printing it. You have really learned a great deal. Of course, you can see that there are more icons and menus. However, this is a good beginning. You can always type up some other note and play with those words to see what the other buttons do!

By the way, if you would like to see what my letter looks like after all the changes, here it is (and I did a "copy" and "paste" to move it here!).

The Most Important Section in This Book: SAVE SAVE SAVE

To begin to save something, it is easiest to have a new "piece of paper" or your "letterhead" open and ready to use in front of you. If you are already in the word-processing part of AppleWorks, all you have to do

Dear Doris,

I am happy to hear that all is well and that you had a lovely holiday in the country. I can imagine that the garden must look wonderful after all the rain you had last month. I hope that your visitors from Switzerland appreciated all the work and preparation that went into this.

Everything is fine here. <u>I have been totally occupied—day and night—with my newest "toy."</u> I bought myself a COMPUTER! I know you will think I am crazy, but I really wanted to communicate with Beth and Paul on a regular basis, and they tell me that the best way to do this is to "e-mail" them. I also want to be able to make corrections easily when typing a letter rather than redoing everything several times because I forgot a line. In addition, you would not believe the fun I am having looking up things on the "World Wide Web."

Then my friend Silvia told me about some wonderful games that I can play on the computer. I am sometimes up late at night unable to stop until I "beat" the computer. I know it sounds silly, but my orthopedic surgeon told me the computer is as good as knitting for arthritis prevention, and I really think that the games are helping me keep my fingers and hands more flexible.

Let me know what you think of all this. More importantly, if you have an "e-mail" address, please send it to me. Think of all the money we will save on postage and telephone calls if we use the Internet! Well, that is all for now.

Love,

The First Week with My New iMac

is point the cursor on the first icon from the left, which looks like a piece of paper with the letter "A" on it. An even better approach is to have an icon of your own such as your letterhead, fax sheet, or plain piece of paper sitting on your desktop for easy access. Then, by pressing the mouse button twice (double-clicking), a window will open that is nothing more than "a blank piece of paper."

Notice that at the top of the window you have the title bar, which at the moment says "untitled (WP)." Above that is the menu bar, a gray horizontal line, and just below that is the button bar with icons. The line below that is the text format bar, which gives you a variety of options and controls for use in the document itself (including the size and typeface you wish to use, whether it is bold, underlined, in color, etc., etc.). Below that you have another format bar for justification, spacing, tabs, etc., and below that you have the "ruler," which helps you line up things on the page, including indentations, etc.

On the menu bar at the top, go to the "File" menu by pointing the cursor on the word "File" and pressing the mouse button once (clicking). A menu will drop down. Find the item that says "Save As." Highlight and open this by pointing the cursor on the item and pressing the mouse button (clicking) (see figure 9.7). Note that the key command for this is to simultaneously hold down the "shift" key, the "Command" key, and the "S" key (⇧+⌘+S).

Figure 9.7

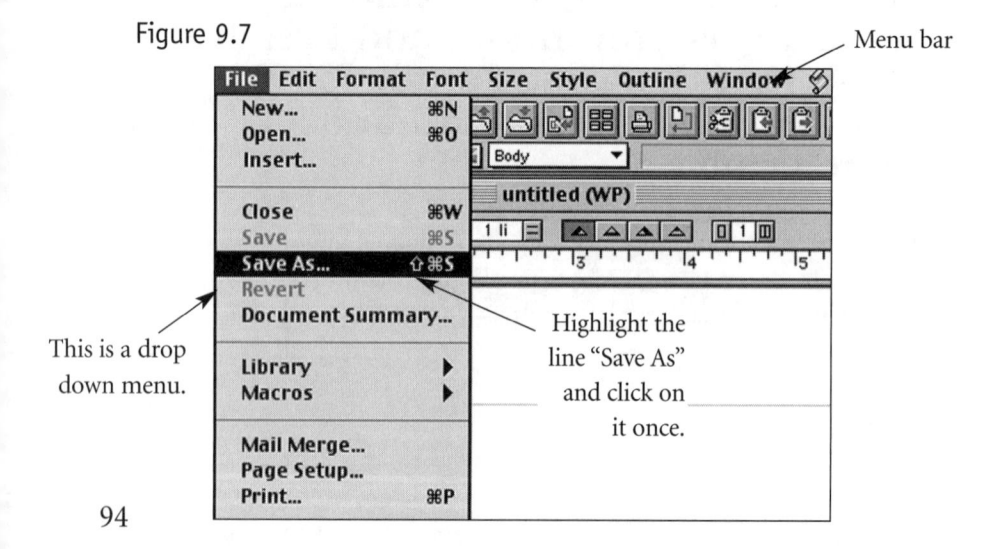

Writing Documents and Correspondence

A new window will open with "Save As" on the lower left of the box with a *highlighted* rectangle that says "untitled" in it. This is a dialog box (see figure 9.8). The first thing you should do is to name your document. To do this just start typing your own words. The highlighted word will disappear automatically when you begin typing. (Remember to try and pick something that will be really *meaningful* when you want to find the document in the future!)The rectangle above this gives you choices of what program or application you want to use. It should be in AppleWorks. DO NOT CHANGE THIS RIGHT NOW.

Figure 9.8

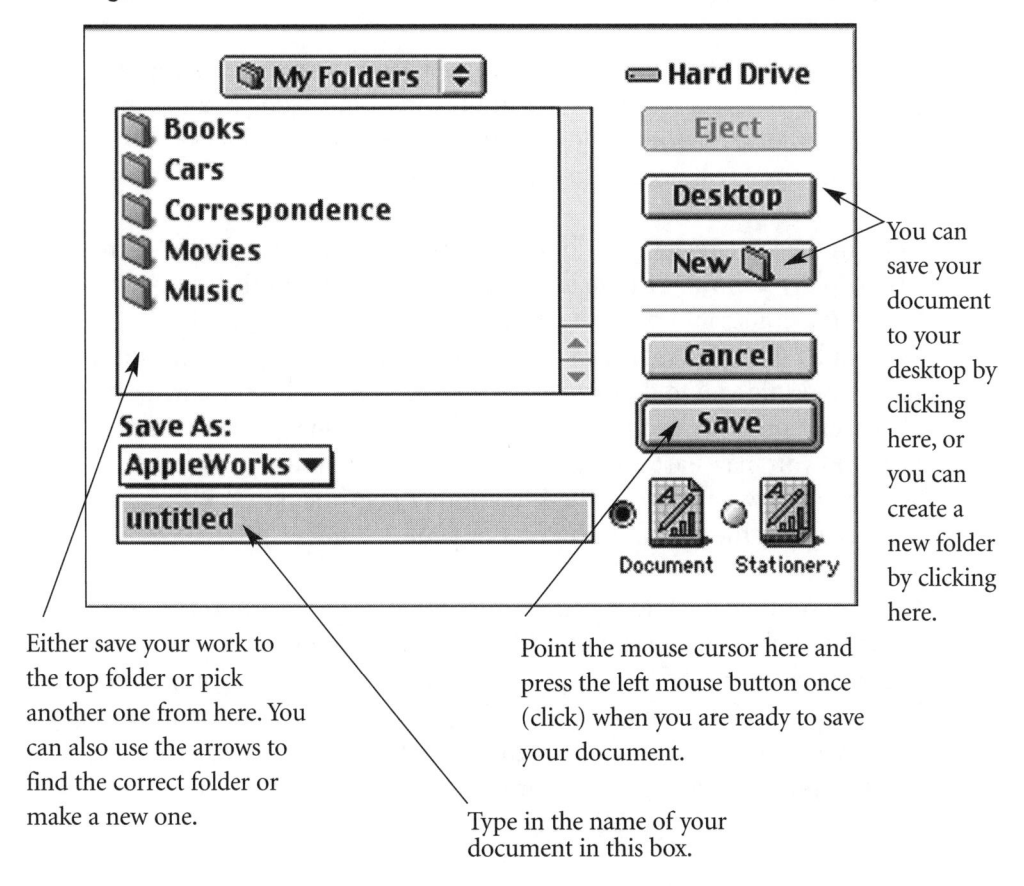

You can save your document to your desktop by clicking here, or you can create a new folder by clicking here.

Either save your work to the top folder or pick another one from here. You can also use the arrows to find the correct folder or make a new one.

Point the mouse cursor here and press the left mouse button once (click) when you are ready to save your document.

Type in the name of your document in this box.

95

The First Week with My New iMac

After you give your document a name, you will need to decide what folder you want it to go into. Let's say you are keeping a folder devoted to your grandchild, Beth. This letter is a thank you note for all the help she gave you in setting up the computer. Therefore, you will want to place it in a folder named "Beth." (With this as an example, you might want to name your file "Beth-computer help-thanks.")

Your folder with the name "Beth" should be sitting in the larger folder called "My Documents." (I hope all this was set up by your helpful young person or the computer expert you hired after reading Chapter 1. If not, look in Chapter 11.)

How do you get to the folder in which you want to save something? If for some reason the gray rectangle at the top of the dialog box has the title of the correct folder, congratulations—you really are lucky! Most of the time you will need to find the correct folder.

Look in the large rectangular box below this gray rectangle. Is the name of the folder you want to use in there? If it is, then point the cursor at the correct folder and press the mouse button twice (double-click). This folder will now appear in the gray rectangle. If you gave your file a name (as I told you to do first thing), you can now point the cursor on "Save" and press the mouse button (click). The dialog box will disappear and you may start typing your letter. (Note that in this example, your title bar will now read "Beth-computer help-thanks (WP)" because this is the title and program of your document.)

If you do not see the folder you wish to use, it might be just one level up or down from the group of folders you are currently seeing. To move up or down one level, point the cursor on the arrows immediately to the right of the top gray rectangle. Press the mouse button once, and a new level of folders will appear. If the folder you wish to use is there, point the cursor on the desired folder and press the mouse button once (click) (see figure 9.9).

If you still can't find the right folder, try going down one level. By now you will have found the correct folder for whatever it is that you are

Writing Documents and Correspondence

working on. The point is that it is important to try to save your work in the proper place so that you can find it again—and find it quickly! The computer is your file cabinet and you do not want to just throw all the papers into one big drawer! (Remember how you hate looking for your tax receipts, your birth certificate, your glasses, and the car keys.)

Figure 9.9

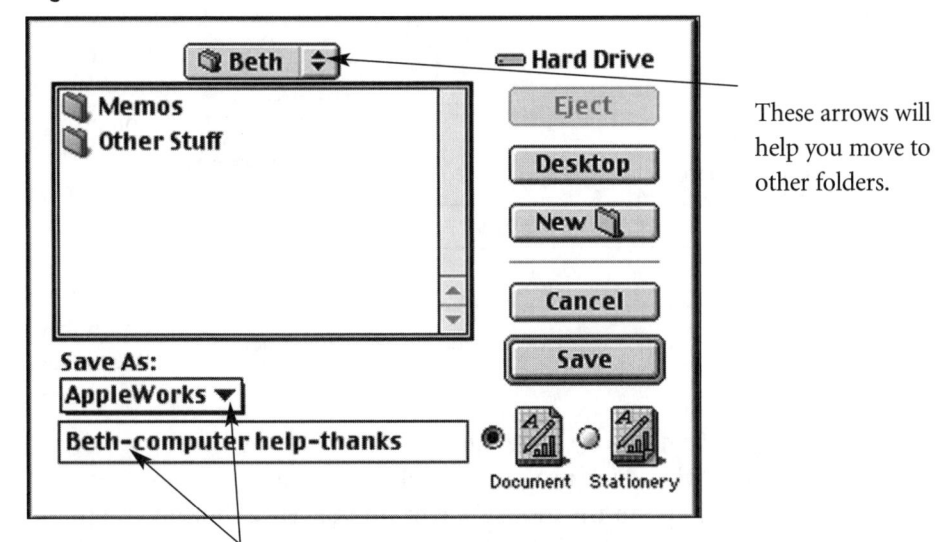

These arrows will help you move to other folders.

When you save your document, these boxes will display the type of document you are saving (in this case, Appleworks) and the name you have given your document (Beth-computer help-thanks).

Now you do have other choices. You may decide that this is something that you want available all the time, so you might want to keep it on your desktop. Look to the right and see where this button is. By clicking on this button, the desktop becomes the place where your document will be saved. (I warn you about doing this too often, however, because it means you will find yourself with three dozen folders scattered everywhere!) There is also a button that allows you to create a new folder, just under the "Desktop" button. Just follow the dialog box questions to create this folder within your main document folder (see figure 9.10).

97

The First Week with My New iMac

Figure 9.10

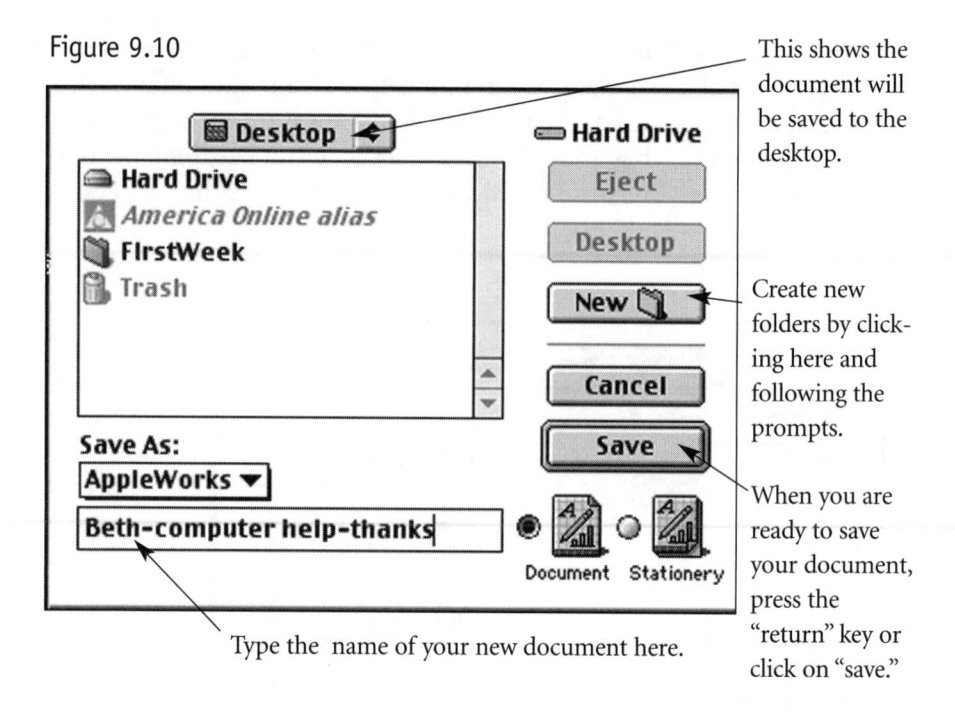

```
        [ Desktop ▼ ]              ⊂═ Hard Drive        This shows the
                                                        document will
   ⊂═ Hard Drive              [    Eject    ]           be saved to the
   🅰 America Online alias                              desktop.
   📁 FirstWeek               [   Desktop   ]
   🗑 Trash
                              [    New 📁  ]            Create new
                                                        folders by click-
                                                        ing here and
                              [   Cancel    ]           following the
                                                        prompts.
   Save As:                   [    Save     ]
   [ AppleWorks ▼ ]                                     When you are
   [ Beth-computer help-thanks ]   ● 📄  ○ 📄           ready to save
                                   Document Stationery  your document,
                                                        press the
        Type the name of your new document here.       "return" key or
                                                        click on "save."
```

When you have named your document, determined where you want it saved, and within which program it will be used, just press the "return" key. Or you can point the mouse cursor on the "Save" button and press the mouse button once (click). Remember, if you want to get out of this dialog box without performing any action either press the "esc" key or point the mouse cursor on the "Cancel" button and press the mouse button once (click). However, I strongly urge you to save your work. It cannot hurt to save everything. You can think about it later and delete it if necessary.

On a lighter note, there is another way of "writing" something as a quick note to yourself that actually saves itself automatically. This is a small program called "Stickies" and you will find it at the bottom of your "Apple" menu. By pointing the mouse cursor on this word at the bottom of the "Apple" menu and clicking, you will get information on how to leave yourself "little reminders" that can be placed anywhere on your desktop. You can even print out your notes.

Chapter 10

Everything Else, Including Other Ways to Get Information and Have Fun, or, What Do I Do with All These CDs and Did I Have to Pay Extra for All This Stuff?

Your computer comes with a number of programs and compact disks that you will probably never use. They are "bundled" together, so in a sense you did not pay extra for these things. But at the same time, the computer company will not give you a rebate if you do not want them!

The First Week with My New iMac

Among the CDs that you received, there will probably be a movie for children. If you are a grandparent reading this book, you will enjoy having this disk as entertainment. However, what is more important is that it is a way of showing you one of the great features of your new computer—DVD. Essentially, what this means is that you can watch CDs of real movies on your computer just as you may currently watch videotapes of movies on your television. With most DVD-CDs you will just load the CD into the CD drive (see Chapter 11 if you are not sure how to do this or see below), point the mouse cursor at the "Apple" menu on the top left of the menu bar, and press the mouse button once (click) on the Apple DVD Player. Then use the controller that appears in the "viewer" window to play the movie. Note that all the controls can also be accessed from the menu bar. Also, for easier viewing, the controller can either be removed (go to "Window" on your menu bar, highlight "Hide Controller," and press the mouse button once [click]) or move to another part of the screen (hold down the cursor on the "Apple" symbol at the top of the device and drag it to a new location). Experiment with all the buttons. This is *really* a lot of fun! (If the movie does not start playing or you do not see the Controller, then check Chapter 11 for step-by-step directions or go to Appendix A, Troubleshooting. Also, for information on renting DVDs over the Internet, see Appendix C, Entertainment, Movies.)

Another great item that *may* come with the computer is a software program that is an encyclopedia (such as *World Book* or *Encarta*). If not, it is well worth purchasing. Something that I still do not understand is how all the information on a whole bookshelf can be "put on" something the size of one or two compact disks. But it does not matter how they do it—the fact is that all *you* have to do is put the *World Book Encyclopedia* CD into your CD drive and watch what happens!

Within a moment, there will be a new icon on the desktop. Point the mouse cursor at this icon and press the mouse button twice (double-click). Then double-click on the World Book installer icon. Follow the instructions and answer the questions, including entering the CD-Key number that is on the outside of the envelope within which you found the *World Book* CD. When everything is installed properly you will see

Everything Else

a dialog box that confirms this. Press the "return" key. Now you will see the World Book icon in its own folder. Double-click on this icon.

The screen will fill with a lovely picture (see figure 10.1). You will then have a new screen with a number of options. You can either browse generally through the encyclopedia or you can search for a particular topic. Once you have opened a particular item, there is something interesting to note. This program has its own special icons at the top of the window. Each one can be identified or defined by pointing the mouse cursor at it and seeing its "title." (**Note:** As with most programs, you can always return to the beginning by going to the "home page." In this case, you point the mouse cursor at the red house and press the mouse button once [click]. Now you can start over.)

Each item gives its own guide or tutorial at the beginning, so do not be afraid to just press different icons and see what happens! However, while it is always interesting to try something for fun, I also understand that you might just want to look something up. With that in mind, point the cursor at the top right where it says "Topics" and press the mouse button once (click). You can then type in the word or name of whatever you want and press the "return" key (or click on the word "Go"). On the left side of the window, you will soon see a list of a number of articles on your subject. Point the cursor on the desired article, press the mouse button twice (double-click), and new information will appear on the right side of the window. Just use your arrow keys to move down the page to read the whole article.

Also note that on the right side of the window there are several choices of how you can search for your information. You are not limited to the encyclopedia CD, but can sometimes go to a number of Web sites "on-line" to get more information. In addition, some of the articles have sound effects and links to related articles. Experiment with any topic that interests you. I particularly enjoy quick access to so many excellent maps and the different "Timelines" that are offered.

Remember, you can always close the program by opening the "File" menu, highlighting the word "Quit," and clicking on it. Alternatively,

The First Week with My New iMac

you can hold down the "Command" key while pressing the letter "Q" and then release both. I strongly urge you to just spend a few minutes playing with this CD. It is good practice, intellectual entertainment, and a lot of fun! You cannot lose information or wipe out anything that is on your CD. You can open as many windows or ask to find as many things as you want. It is another great way of getting to know how to make your computer work for you.

Figure 10.1

The *World Book Encyclopedia*

This might be a good time to remind you how to "load" and "unload" your CD from the drive. I hope your helpful young person has shown you where the drive is, but chances are you have already figured this out. After all, it is rather obvious that there is a narrow slit in the front of the computer between the two speakers!

On the front of the computer, just below the screen of the monitor is an oval slot that is framed in the main color of your computer. To load a CD, place the disk—the side with words facing up—at the opening of the slit and gently press it in slightly. The drive will take hold of the disk and "swallow" it all by itself.

Everything Else

To remove a CD, close all the open windows that are connected to the CD. You need to see only the icon on the desktop. Point the mouse cursor on the icon, hold down the mouse button, and drag the icon to the trash can. (While you are doing this you will only see a ghosted image of the icon moving. When you release the mouse button, the icon will drop into the trash and then the disk will eject itself from the CD drive.) Alternatively, press the "Command" key and the "E" key simultaneously (⌘+E) or point the mouse cursor on the word "Special" on the menu bar, go down to "Eject," and click. (If this does not work, see Appendix A, Troubleshooting.)

While we are discussing loading and unloading CDs, I should mention that you can use your computer and the CD drive to listen to audio compact disks while you work. If you place an audio CD into the CD drive, it should start playing right away. Obviously, there is only one CD drive so you cannot listen to music while you are using other disks like the encyclopedia or Scrabble. However, for most other things it is nice to have the entertainment. Go to Chapter 11 for complete details on how to play an audio CD and control the volume.

Another Special CD for Your Enjoyment—iMovie®

In the orange iMac envelope there is one more special CD that is worth mentioning here. For some people, it is one of the major reasons they bought this computer. The CD is called iMovie and it will allow you to edit your own home videos. In fact, the program is already loaded on your hard drive, and this is just a disk to reload the program in case your computer "crashes."

To open this program, point the mouse cursor on the "Macintosh" icon and double-click. Point the mouse cursor on the "Applications" folder and press the mouse button twice (double-click). Use the arrow keys to highlight the iMovie folder, or point the mouse cursor on this icon and double-click. This is one program where I strongly urge you to do the special "tutorial" and also read the section titled "iMovie Read Me." It really is important and will increase your knowledge and, therefore,

The First Week with My New iMac

your pleasure. The first thing you need to do *after* opening the iMovie icon is to also click on the "Help" menu and open the iMovie tutorial item that is seen there. Just follow along and learn the best way to do different tasks. This is really an instance where the tutorial's picture is worth more than my thousand words!

Sherlock® 2—Your New Best Friend

Sherlock (or Sherlock 2) is one of the better programs in your computer because it will help you find "things." It can do everything from finding information on the Internet to finding your lost files. (I personally wish I had something like this in real life to find my keys and glasses while answering my questions about the garden!) To get Sherlock to work for you either press the "Command" key and the "F" key simultaneously (⌘+F) or point the mouse cursor on the "magnifying glass" icon on your desktop and press the mouse button twice (double-click).

If you wish to find something in your computer like a folder or file, type the name of this item in the narrow rectangular box where the cursor is blinking. Then point the mouse cursor on the magnifying glass to the right and press the mouse button once (click) or press the "return" key. Note that you can also customize your search by selecting from the buttons just below the rectangle and magnifying glass.

If you wish to search normal reference guides, like the dictionary, thesaurus, or encyclopedia, you need to be "on-line," so sign on to your Internet Service Provider (ISP), point the mouse cursor on the icon that looks like books, and click. Type in the item you need checked and press the "return" key or click on the magnifying glass to the right.

While you are "on-line," you can also search the Internet by pointing the mouse cursor on the icon that looks like a globe and clicking once. This will bring up a number of "search engines." You can select whichever one you prefer (or use several) to help you find just about anything! For example, if you type in the words "scuba diving equipment," a list of 76 sites will appear. By pointing your mouse cursor on

Everything Else

one of these, a description of that site will appear at the bottom of the window. (Note that there are also underlined words in blue showing the direct "link." By clicking on the link you will go directly to that site.) You can also note the actual Web address of the site or go to it immediately by clicking on the site as you point to it.

Other areas that can be accessed by Sherlock while you are on-line include shopping, news, people, and your own personal interests that have been picked as favorites. Go ahead and play with your new best friend and explore an easy way to have fun and get results.

All the Other Things That Have Not Yet Been Discussed

Here we are near the end of the book, and you are probably wondering why I have not mentioned some task or program that really interests you. Well, there are a whole lot of reasons for that, including the fact that this is my book and this is what I thought was most useful! In addition, I would imagine that you have looked in the Troubleshooting section (Appendix A) or Chapter 11, and you have seen whether your topic might be mentioned there. Such things as the correct way to "Shut Down" your computer and the way to wake it up are all mentioned in simple, easy-to-follow instructions there.

As for all the other things that really have not been discussed, I have several thoughts about this. There are many different computer books on the market. It is my feeling that if you feel comfortable with all the items covered in this book, you are ready to try one of those big, thick books. You might find them a bit intimidating after reading this book. However, all you need to do is look in the index for a keyword that covers your question. Then just read those few paragraphs or that section. If you have gone all through this book, you have the skills and the vocabulary to understand most things that the big boys will throw at you! In particular I would recommend a book by Maria Langer titled *MAC OS® 9*, published by Peachpit Press, and *Sad Macs, Bombs, and Other Disasters* by Ted Landau. If your iMac has not "crashed," you will also be able to find help on the Web (see Appendix C).

105

The First Week with My New iMac

My other thought is that this is a basic, introductory book on computers. Nonetheless, it has given you a lot of information. If you choose only to work and play with the items I have covered, you will be doing an awful lot. In some cases, you will be using your computer more than the majority of people I know! (Maybe some of my friends should buy this book so they can get more use out of their expensive machines.)

Whatever you decide, never let a book or a person intimidate you. It is your computer, and you can use it any way you want!

Chapter 11
A *Step-by-Step* Guide for Each Task

How to Connect All the New Equipment

The different components of your system will all plug into the back or side of your monitor. (This is the thing that looks like a television and is both the viewing screen and the brains of your system.) Refer to the diagram that came with your assembly instructions as you follow the directions below.

1. Do not plug anything into an electrical outlet at this time!

2. Take the cord from the keyboard and plug it into the "USB" port on the side of the monitor. It is a rectangular plug that goes into a similar rectangular port on the monitor. (Check the diagram sent with the computer and the instructions.)

3. Take the cord from the mouse (the round item that is the size of the palm of your hand with a ball on its underside) and plug it into the rectangular "USB" port on the keyboard. (Check the diagram sent with the computer.)

4. Take the cord that looks like a thick, colorful power cord and connect one end to the back of the monitor. (The other end will soon go into a surge protector and then into an electrical outlet.) Do not force anything—that means do not press too hard. With moderate pressure you can push this plug into the port.

5. The printer has two cables that need to be attached and connected. One is black and has an electrical plug on one end and a "female" connector with two holes in it on the other end. Plug the female connector into the back of your printer. (Wait to plug the other end into the surge protector, which then goes into an electrical outlet.) The other cable is another "USB" cable, which is plugged first into the printer and then into the keyboard.

A *Step-by-Step* Guide for Each Task

6. Your modem is internal (it came with the computer and is inside the monitor), so you need to connect one end of the telephone cord to the side of the monitor (to the left of the "USB" ports) and the other end to a telephone jack. If a telephone jack is not close by, get a telephone extension cord. (See the list of things to do while you wait in Chapter 2!)

7. If you have decided to purchase an external (not built-in) back-up disk drive, this should be plugged into the "USB" port that is still available on the side of the monitor. The reason for plugging it into this "USB" port is that it does not have its own power supply and needs the computer's power to operate.

8. Now it is time to plug everything (monitor and printer) into an electrical outlet. You must plug these power cords into three-pronged (grounded) outlets. It is best to plug them into a surge protector and then plug the surge protector into the grounded outlet. A surge protector usually looks like an extension cord with a rectangular strip of outlets, a rocker switch, and a light to show that there is power. This will protect your expensive equipment from electrical mishaps. Just ask the person at the hardware or the computer store to help you find one that meets your needs.

How to Add the Printer

Your printer will come with an installation CD, so place the disk in the CD drive and wait for it to "turn on." A window will appear in front of you. Just point the cursor at the appropriate answer "button" (usually "Yes" or "Next") and press the mouse button once (click) to answer each question as it appears. When you come to the last window, point the cursor at the word "Finish" and press the mouse button (click on the "Finish" button). The printer is now installed. If the computer then tells you that it needs to restart itself, press the "return" key or point the mouse cursor at the "OK" and press the mouse button once (click).

109

The First Week with My New iMac

How to Add a Disk Drive

The iMac does not come with an internal device for saving your work onto disks that can be removed from the machine and stored in a separate place for safekeeping. There are people who do not believe in keeping "backups" of their work or are happy to have one copy of their work saved to the internal hard drive of the computer. This is not my philosophy. I think that it is important to save your work. The advantage of having it on some kind of disk is that it is a way to recover your work if something goes wrong with your iMac, and it allows you to move your information to other computers if you want to share your work.

Whatever type of disk drive you buy:

1. Read the directions that come with this hardware.

2. Understand that in order to have enough power to operate this hardware you will need to "plug it into" one of the USB connections on the side of the iMac.

3. Whatever you currently have plugged into the second USB connection (like your printer) will have to be plugged into the USB connection on the keyboard.

How to Load and Unload CDs
Loading a CD

On the front of the computer, just below the screen of the monitor, is an oval slot that is framed in the main color of your computer. To load a CD:

1. Place the disk—the side with words goes up—at the opening of the slit and gently press it in slightly.

2. The drive will take hold of the disk and "swallow" it all by itself.

Ejecting a Disk

To remove a CD, close all the open windows that are connected to the CD. You need to see only the CD icon on the desktop.

1. Point the mouse cursor on the icon, hold down the mouse button, and drag the icon to the trash can. (While you are doing this you will only see a ghosted image of the icon moving. When you release the mouse button, the icon will drop into the trash and the CD will eject itself from the CD drive.)

2. Alternatively, press the "Command" key and the "E" key simultaneously (⌘+E). *or*

3. Point the mouse cursor on the word "Special" on the menu bar, go down to "Eject," and press the mouse button (click).

4. If none of this works, see Appendix A as your last resort!

Turning the Computer On— Turning the Computer Off

To Turn On the Computer

1. Be sure the computer is plugged into a surge protector, and that the surge protector is plugged into an electrical outlet.

2. Be sure the keyboard cable is connected to the monitor, and the mouse cable is connected to the keyboard.

3. Press the large button on the front right side of the monitor; and a light will come on. (The universal symbol for power is ⏻ and that symbol will be on all power buttons or controls.) *or*

4. Press the round button on the top right side of the keyboard that also has the universal symbol for power [⏻].

5. Wait while the computer turns itself on—your desktop will appear in a minute or two.

The First Week with My New iMac

6. While you wait there will be a smiling face in the "Welcome" window on the monitor screen and then flashing icons at the bottom. THIS IS NORMAL. It is called "booting." Just wait.

7. If the computer "beeps" at you, read what it says and follow the instructions. Usually it needs you to hit the "return" key to continue (or point the mouse cursor at the word "Done" and press the mouse button once [click]). When you see the desktop you are ready to begin.

To Turn Off the Computer—or Restart It or Put It into Sleep Mode

1. Close any "open" windows by pointing the cursor on the small square at the top left of each window called the "Close" box. (Look at the horizontally striped title bar. It is all the way on the left all by itself.)

2. Press the power button on the upper right side of the keyboard (the one that has the universal power symbol [⏻]).

3. There will be a "bing" sound (or whatever sound you have chosen), and then you are given several choices (see figure 11.1).

4. Press the "return" key if you want to "Shut Down," which means you are turning it off completely.

5. If the initial command to press the power button was a mistake, then press the "esc" key to cancel the command.

6. If you just want to keep the iMac on but in "Sleep" mode, point the mouse cursor on the second button from the left and press the mouse button once (click). "Sleep" mode is a power-saving feature. It allows you to start working again where you left off with everything saved to memory.

A *Step-by-Step* Guide for Each Task

7. If you want to "Restart" the computer (also known as "rebooting") then point the mouse cursor at the button all the way to the left and press the mouse button once (click).

8. The alternative method is to:

   - Go to the menu bar and point the mouse cursor on the word "Special" (see figure 11.2).

   - Press and hold down the mouse button;

   - Drag the mouse cursor down to the command you wish to perform ("Restart," "Sleep," or "Shut Down") and release the mouse button.

Figure 11.1

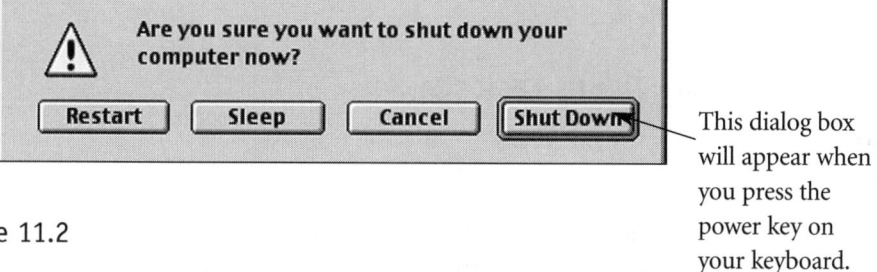

This dialog box will appear when you press the power key on your keyboard.

Figure 11.2

You can also shut down by selecting the "Special" pull-down menu and highlighting "Shut Down."

113

The First Week with My New iMac

The Control Panels: How to Change Settings

The Control Panels include some important items that allow you to change the default settings and customize your computer. You can access the Control Panels using either the mouse or keyboard commands. For keyboard commands see page 117.

These icons let you make the following adjustments:

- Mouse: the speed at which the cursor (pointer) moves and how quickly you need to press the button.

- Display: the look of the desktop and windows, screen-savers, etc.

- Fonts.

- Sounds: the noises that the computer makes when it does certain tasks.

- Date and Time.

To Make Things Easier to See

1. Icons

- Look at the top line on the desktop with the "Apple" symbol on the left and five words next to it. This is the menu bar.

- Point the mouse cursor on the word "View" on the menu bar and press the mouse button once (click).

- Point the mouse cursor on the term "View Options" and press the mouse button once (click).

- Change the size of the icons by pointing the cursor at the button you prefer and clicking to select it.

- Point the mouse cursor on the "OK" button and press the mouse button once (click).

A *Step-by-Step* Guide for Each Task

2. Monitor

- Point the mouse cursor on the "Apple" menu and click to bring down the menu.
- Highlight and click on "Control Panels."

- Point the mouse cursor on the "Monitors" icon in the "Control Panels" window and press the mouse button twice (double-click), or use the arrow keys to highlight the icon and then double-click on it.

- On the right side of the window go to "Resolution" and change the setting to "640 x 480, 117Hz."

- Change whatever other settings you choose, such as "Contrast" and "Brightness."

- Close the window by pointing the mouse cursor on the small square in the upper left corner (the "Close" box) and pressing the mouse button once (clicking) or by pressing the "Command" key and the "W" key at the same time (⌘+W).

3. Mouse

- Point the mouse cursor on the "Apple" menu and click to bring down the menu.

- Highlight and click on "Control Panels."

- Point the mouse cursor on the "Mouse" icon in the "Control Panels" window and press the mouse button twice (double-click) or use the arrow keys to highlight the icon and then double-click on it (see figure 11.3).

- Point the mouse cursor on the colored tab of the control slide and hold down the mouse button while dragging the tab to make adjustments to the speed of the mouse and the speed needed to double-click (see figure 11.4).

115

The First Week with My New iMac

- Close the window by pointing the mouse cursor on the small square in the upper left corner (the "Close" box) and pressing the mouse button once (clicking) or by pressing the "Command" key and the "W" key at the same time (⌘+W).

To Change Other Settings Such as Display, Date and Time, and Sounds

1. Go to the icon on the "Control Panels" window and open that icon by pressing the mouse button twice (double-click).

2. Go through the various choices offered and experiment when there is a "Test" box.

3. Make whatever changes you want.

Figure 11.3

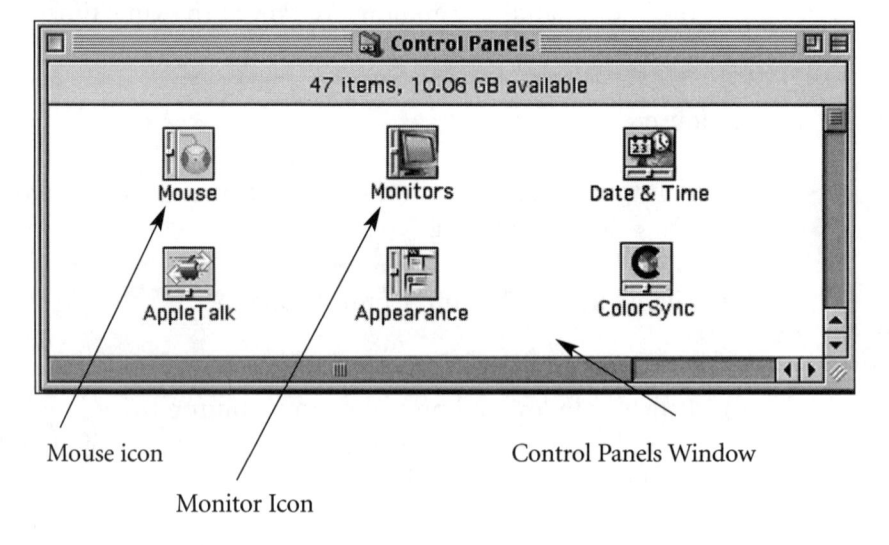

```
                    Control Panels
              47 items, 10.06 GB available

       Mouse          Monitors         Date & Time

      AppleTalk      Appearance        ColorSync
```

Mouse icon   Control Panels Window
      Monitor Icon

116

A *Step-by-Step* Guide for Each Task

4. To end a task, point the cursor at the small square button in the upper left side of the active window (the "Close" box) and press the mouse button once (click).

Figure 11.4

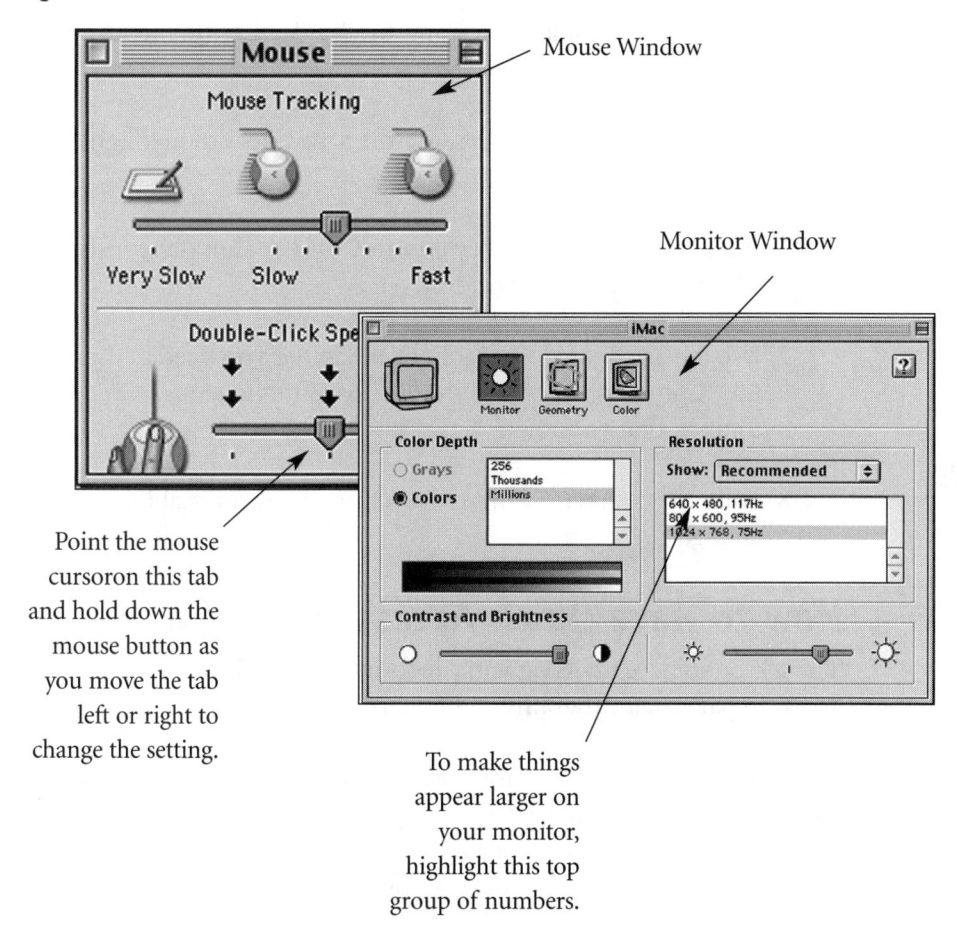

Mouse Window

Monitor Window

Point the mouse cursoron this tab and hold down the mouse button as you move the tab left or right to change the setting.

To make things appear larger on your monitor, highlight this top group of numbers.

117

The First Week with My New iMac

Keyboard Commands

1. Press the "M" key on the keyboard to highlight "Macintosh HD."

2. Press the "Command" key and the "O" key simultaneously (⌘+O) to open the window.

3. Press the "S" key to highlight "System Folder."

4. Press the "Command" key and the "O" key simultaneously (⌘+O) to open the window.

5. Press the "C" key and then use the arrow keys to highlight "Control Panels."

6. Press the "Command" key and the "O" key simultaneously (⌘+O) to open this window.

7. Use the arrow keys to highlight the folder you need and press the "Command" key and the "O" key simultaneously (⌘+O) to open that window.

8. Follow the directions in each section above for making changes.

How to Have Quick Access to Your Work

The reason to have items on your desktop is to provide quick and easy access to particular programs and folders.

As an example imagine you are working on a report about Chinese snuff bottles, and the folder for this report is in another folder called "My Documents." You are working on this report every few days, but it does not need to stay "open" on your desktop.

1. Point the cursor on the "My Documents" icon and press the mouse button twice (double-click).

A *Step-by-Step* Guide for Each Task

2. Look at the window in front of you, point the cursor on the folder that says "Chinese snuff bottles," and click once to highlight it.

Mouse Commands

- Point the mouse cursor on the "File" menu and press the mouse button once (click).

- Point the mouse cursor on "Make Alias" and press the mouse button once (click). *Or*

Keyboard Commands

- Press the "Command" key and the "M" key simultaneously (⌘+M) to make a shortcut or "alias" of this folder.

- Point the mouse cursor at this new folder and hold down the mouse button while you drag it to the desktop. Then release the mouse button.

- This folder is now on the desktop ready to use.

- To open it, point the cursor on the folder and double-click. *or*

- Hold down both the "Command" key and the "option" key while dragging the folder to the new location. An "alias" will appear when you release the mouse button first and then the keys.

119

The First Week with My New iMac

Windows: How to Open, Move, Resize, Scroll, and Close These Things!

To Open a Program or a Folder

1. Point the cursor on the folder or program icon you want and press the mouse button twice (double-click).

2. From this window pick the files or folders that you want to open; follow the procedure above until you have the item you want.

3. Do this once more to open the window with which you want to work.

To Move a Window That Is Covering Up Something, or Just Not Where You Want It to Be

1. Point the cursor on any border of the window.

2. Hold down the mouse button and drag the window to another part of the desktop.

3. Release the mouse button.

4. The window and everything in it will be in the new position.

To Resize a Window So It Is Easier to Work With or See

1. Point the cursor on the lower right corner of the window.

2. Hold down the mouse button and drag the small box of the window to the position that you want.

3. Release the mouse button.

4. This will resize a window "in proportion" (height and width).

A *Step-by-Step* Guide for Each Task

5. If you do not see this box, you cannot resize the window. You will need to move the window to another location to have access to this resizing box to change the shape.

To Scroll Down or Over in a Window to See Everything That Is There

1. If you are not seeing everything in a window, there will be a vertical colored bar to the right and a horizontal colored bar at the bottom of the window.

2. Point the cursor at the up, down, right, or left arrow.

3. Hold down the mouse button to move the contents of the screen in the desired direction.

4. You can also point the cursor anywhere along the scroll bar and press the mouse button (click) to jump ahead to a certain area.

5. One more way to scroll is to point the cursor on the colored bar (or rectangle) *in* the scroll bar. Hold down the mouse button while dragging this box (rectangle) in the direction you want. This scrolls through long documents faster.

To Close a Window

1. Point the cursor at the small square at the top left of the window on the title bar (bar with horizontal striped lines) that is called the "Close" box.

2. Press the mouse button once (click).

Another way to close a window:

1. Press the "Command" key plus the "W" key at the same time (⌘+W). (To close *all* open windows press the "option" key,

The First Week with My New iMac

the "Command" key, and the "W" key simultaneously.)

Still one more way to close a window:

1. Go to and open the "File" menu.

2. Point the mouse cursor on "Close" and press the mouse button once (click).

3. Respond to any dialog box that appears.

Figure 11.5

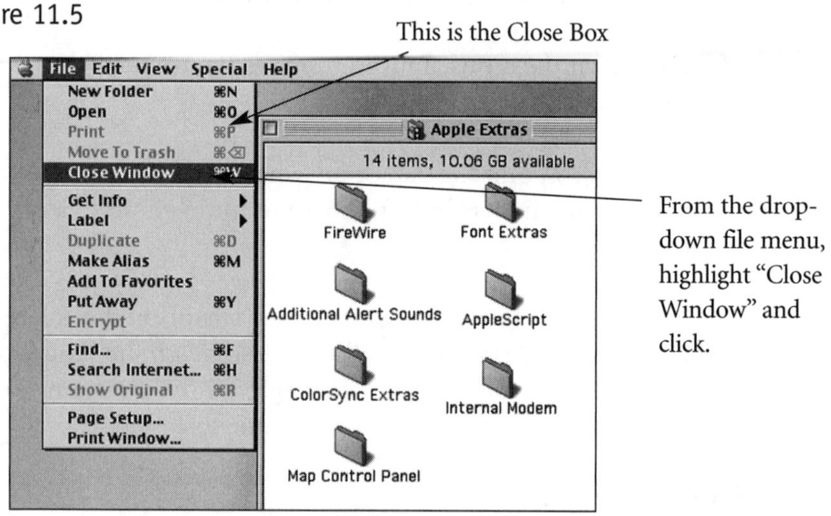

This is the Close Box

From the drop-down file menu, highlight "Close Window" and click.

How to Connect with an Internet Service Provider

1. Point the mouse cursor on the icon that says "Get me on the Internet" and looks like a globe with a connecting plug in a hand.

2. Press the mouse button twice (double-click) and follow the instructions as they appear in this tutorial.

A *Step-by-Step* Guide for Each Task

3. If ever you want to quit one of these tutorials press the "Command" key and the "Q" key simultaneously (⌘+Q).

To Connect to America Online

1. On the desktop find the icon that says "Macintosh HD."

2. Point the cursor on this icon and press the mouse button twice (double-click).

3. Point the cursor at the icon that says "Internet" and double-click.

4. Point the cursor at the icon that says "AOL" and double-click.

5. Instructions for setting up the service will appear on the screen. Follow them!

An alternative method: If you have a CD for America Online, put the disk into your disk drive and follow the instructions.

To Connect to Another Internet Service Provider Such as Microsoft Network®

Follow the instructions above, but choose a different server's icon (if others are preinstalled on your iMac) such as "MSN." Most ISPs offer a free trial period, so you might want to try several to see which works best for you. They can be loaded into the computer with a free CD. Remember, you will need a different e-mail address for each ISP.

How to Receive E-mail

1. Find the icon of your Internet Service Provider (ISP) on the right side of your desktop.

2. Point the cursor on the icon and press the mouse button twice (double-click).

123

The First Week with My New iMac

3. For America Online (AOL), look at the window in front of you, place the cursor in the box that says "Sign On" and press the mouse button twice (double-click). Or simply press the "return" key. **Note:** When you see a button with a double line around it, this is your primary choice. Pressing the "return" key will activate the command and pressing the "esc" key will cancel the command.

4. Wait—and wait some more while the computer's modem connects to the ISP. This can take some time, so relax.

5. Once you are connected, a new window will appear.

6. If you are using AOL, a voice will say, "Welcome" and will tell you if "You've Got Mail."

7. To read your mail, point the cursor on the icon of an open mailbox with a yellow letter in it, and press the mouse button once (click).

8. Look at the folder and the tab that says "New Mail"—use the arrow keys to move down the list and "highlight" the message you want to read.

9. If you want to read the highlighted message, press the "return" key.

10. Read your mail!

How to Reply to E-mail You Have Been Sent
How to Reply to the Person Who Sent You a Message

1. Point the cursor on the icon on the right side of the message box that says "Reply" and press the mouse button once (click). (This icon is at the top of a vertical column of icons. See figure 11.6.)

2. Note that you have a new window with the "Send To" box and the "Subject" box already filled in.

A *Step-by-Step* Guide for Each Task

3. Note that the cursor is blinking in the "message" area. (If you do not see it, press the space bar a few times and it will be more visible.)

4. Write your message.

5. Point the cursor on the icon on the right side that says "Send Now" and press the mouse button once (click).

6. When a box appears that says "Your mail has been sent," acknowledge the computer's statement by pressing the "return" key or pointing the cursor on "OK" and clicking.

How to Forward the Message You Have Just Received to Someone Else

1. Point the cursor on the icon on the right side of the message box that says "Forward" and press the mouse button once (click). (This icon is just below the "Reply" icon in the right vertical column. See figure 11.7.)

2. Note that the cursor is blinking in the "Send To" box. You must fill in the recipient's e-mail address.

3. Either type in the address or go to the "Address Book" icon just to the right of the "Send To" box and press the mouse button once (click).

4. Move the arrow keys up and down to highlight the name of the person to whom you want to forward the message.

5. When the correct name is highlighted press the "Send To" button on the right or double-click on that name.

6. To send the same message to more than one person, use the arrow keys to highlight the next name to whom you wish to send *this* message and double-click on that name. Then close the Address Book by clicking on the "Close" box, the small square on the upper left side of this window's title bar.

The First Week with My New iMac

7. Press the "tab" key *two* times to move the cursor. The cursor will now be blinking in the message box. Fill in the box with a comment or note.

8. Point the cursor on the icon that says "Send Now" and press the mouse button once (click).

9. Respond to the computer's acknowledgment that your message has been sent by pressing the "return" key or pointing the cursor on the "OK" button and pressing the mouse button once (clicking).

Figure 11.6

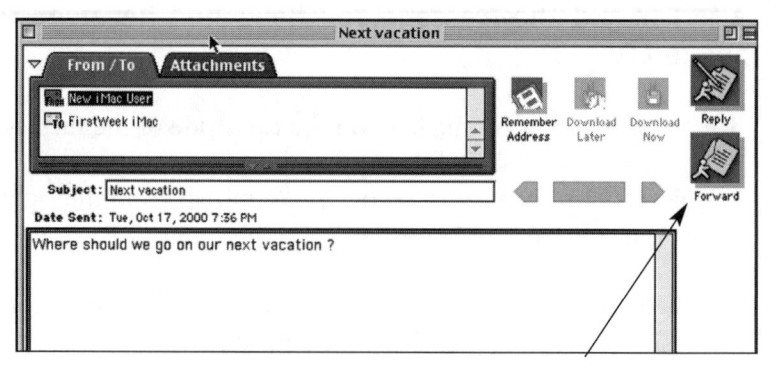

To forward the e-mail you have received to someone else, click on the "Forward" button.

Figure 11.7

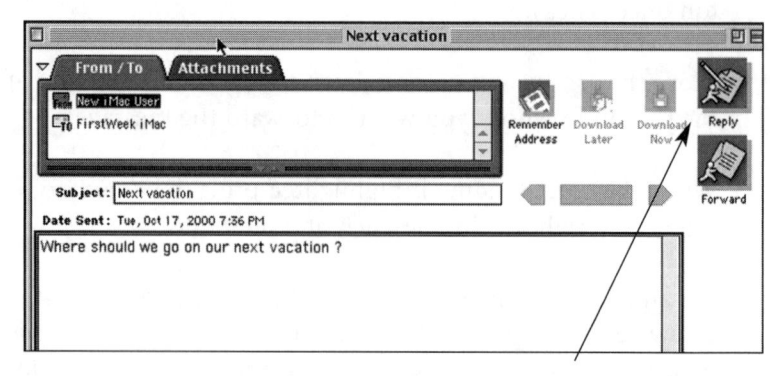

To reply to the person who sent you an e-mail, click on the "Reply" button.

How to Send Your Own E-mail "from Scratch"!

1. There are two ways to get a "fresh piece of paper" on which to write your e-mail message.

   - With the AOL window "active," hold down the "Command" key and the "M" key at the same time and then release both at the same time (⌘+M). Now you see a window in which you can fill in your message. *or*

   - Find the row of icons along the second line from the top. The second one from the left looks like a piece of yellow paper. Point the cursor at that icon, and press the mouse button once (click).

2. The cursor will be blinking in the "Send To" box. Fill in the e-mail address of the person to whom you wish to send mail by typing in the address or "looking it up" in the Address Book.

To fill in the address:

   - Type in the information exactly as it has been given to you. It will include a user name, the "at" symbol (@), and the name of an Internet Service Provider (example: hdl@ibm.net). Do not leave spaces or add extra punctuation. The computer is very fussy about this, unlike the postal service.

To find the address in the Address Book:

   - Point the cursor on the icon that says "Address Book" to the right of the "Send To" box and press the mouse button once (click).

   - Use the arrow keys to find and highlight the name of the person to whom you wish to send e-mail.

The First Week with My New iMac

- Press the "Send To" button or point the mouse cursor on the name and press the mouse button twice (double-click).

- The name should now be in the "Send To" box.

- Close the Address Book by clicking on the "Close" box, the small square on the upper left side.

Follow either procedure to add more names to the "Send To" box.

3. Press the "tab" key to move the cursor to the next box. The cursor is now blinking in the "Subject" box.

4. Fill in a few descriptive words for your recipient.

5. Press the "tab" key again and the cursor is now in the "Message" box. Write your message.

6. When finished, point the cursor on the icon on the right that says "Send Now" and press the mouse button once (click).

7. Respond to the computer's notification that "Your mail has been sent" by pressing the "return" key or pointing the cursor on "OK" and pressing the mouse button once (clicking).

Note: If you are *not* "signed on," the icon that says "Send Now" will be shaded and nothing will happen when you "click" on the icon. Your options are to click on "Send Later" or to be "on-line" when writing your mail. If you have unlimited monthly usage, this is not a problem. Otherwise you may wish to compose mail, click on the "Send Later" icon, and the next time you are signed on, follow the procedure outlined on the next page.

A *Step-by-Step* Guide for Each Task

How to Send Mail in the "Waiting To Be Sent" Folder

1. Compose mail "off-line." Point the cursor on "Send Later" and press the mouse button once (click).

2. "Sign on" and wait until you are connected.

3. Point the mouse cursor at the "Mail Center" icon (third from the left on second row) and press the mouse button once (click).

4. Drag the mouse cursor down to the second item from the bottom, "Mail Waiting To Be Sent" and press the mouse button once (click). (See figure 11.8.)

Figure 11.8

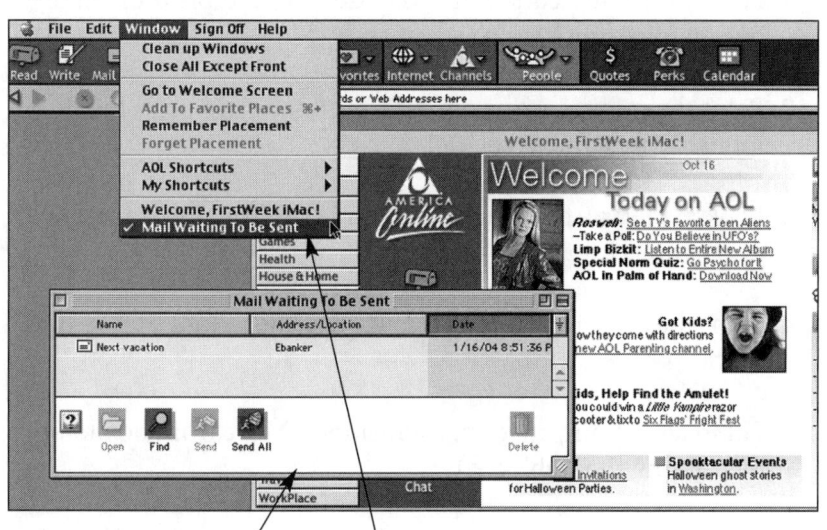

This is the "Mail Waiting To Be Sent" window. Click on the button that you want to send one or all of your e-mails.

AOL's Welcome Window with the Mail center drop-down menu

129

The First Week with My New iMac

5. If you want to send one message, highlight the message by clicking on it, point the cursor on the "Send" icon, and press the mouse button once (click).

6. Do the same for each message that you want to "Send Now." *or*

7. Point the mouse cursor on the "Send All" icon, press the mouse button once, and watch all the messages disappear!

8. Close this window by clicking on the small square in the upper left corner of this window (the "Close" box).

How to Set Up Your Address Book

First, open America Online. To do this go to the desktop, point the cursor at the AOL icon, and press the mouse button twice (double-click).

1. Point the mouse cursor on "Mail Center" and press the mouse button once (click).

2. Point the mouse cursor on "Address Book" and press the mouse button once (click).

3. Look at lower left of window to find the "New Person" icon (see figure 11.9).

4. Point the cursor on this icon and press the mouse button once (click).

5. Fill in all the information. (Remember: Move from box to box by pressing the "tab" key.)

6. Press the "return" key or point the cursor on the "OK" button and click.

7. Your Address Book now contains this person's e-mail address.

8. Repeat this to add other names.

A *Step-by-Step* Guide for Each Task

9. If you wish to have a group mailing find the "New Group" icon.

   - Give the group a name like "All the Children" or "Women Friends."

   - Fill in each person's e-mail address in the boxes.

   - Press the "return" key.

   - When you wish to send something to all the children, highlight this "name" in your Address Book and press the "Send To" button. The addresses of all the children will not appear in the "Send To" box; however, everyone will be sent the message.

Figure 11.9

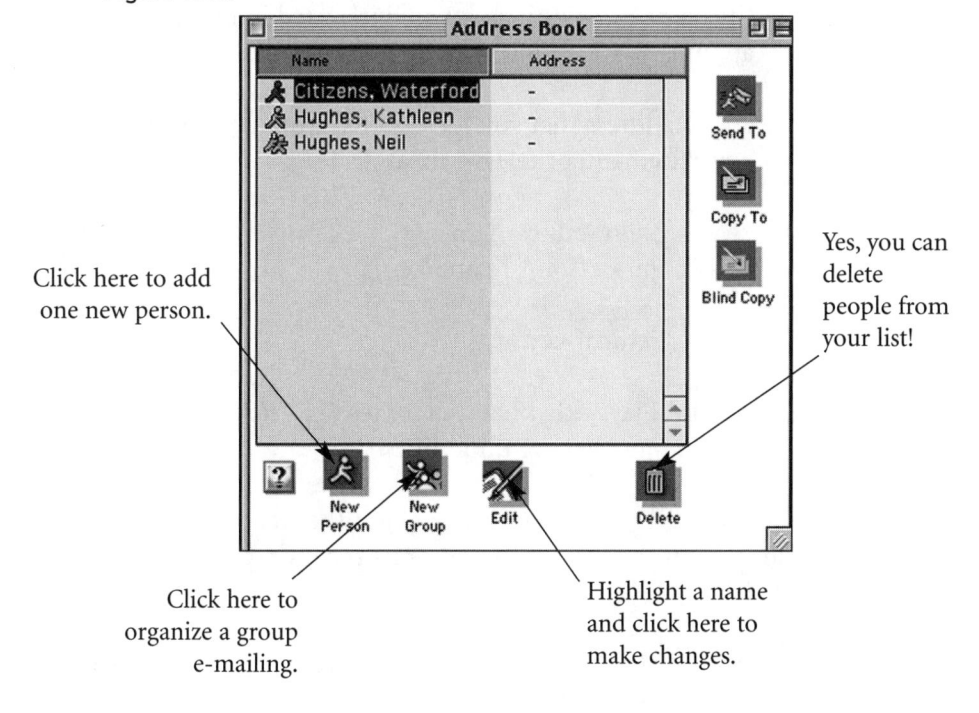

Click here to add one new person.

Click here to organize a group e-mailing.

Highlight a name and click here to make changes.

Yes, you can delete people from your list!

131

The First Week with My New iMac

How to Get on the Internet

1. On the desktop, point the cursor at the AOL icon and press the mouse button twice (double-click).

2. "Sign on" and wait until you are connected. *Keep waiting—* remember this could take some time!

3. On the lowest bar (third bar down just above the title bar) look for a white rectangle that says, "Type Search words, Keywords or Web Addresses here."

4. Point the cursor in this box and press the mouse button once (click) to highlight the box.

5. Type:

   - the name of anything you are interested in knowing more about;

   - a Web address that you have gotten from an article, an advertisement, or television; and

   - "www." followed by the name of a company or organization and ".com" or ".org" as appropriate.

6. Press the "return" key.

7. Have fun! Play with whatever comes up. Click on "links" (items in blue that are underlined).

8. If you want to go back a page, point the cursor on the back arrow (on the third bar) and press the mouse button once (click).

9. To Stop: Point the cursor on the small square in the upper left corner of the window (the "Close" box) and press the mouse button once (click).

A *Step-by-Step* Guide for Each Task

An alternative method:

1. Sign on with your Internet Service Provider.

2. Point the mouse cursor on the icon "Sherlock 2" that looks like a magnifying glass and press the mouse button twice (double-click).
3. Point the mouse cursor on the icon that looks like the globe and press the mouse button once (click) (see figure 11.10).

4. Type in a keyword and press the "return" key, or point the mouse cursor on the magnifying glass icon to the right and press the mouse button once (click).

5. See all the options that multiple "search engines" have found along with the Web addresses.

6. Point the mouse cursor on one of these and double-click.

7. Wait as that Web site is accessed.

How to Follow the Stock Market over the Internet

Using America Online (AOL) as your ISP:

1. On the desktop, point the cursor at the AOL icon and press the mouse button twice (double-click).

2. "Sign on" and wait until you are connected.

3. On the left side of the "Welcome" window, find the "Personal Finance" item and click on it.

4. Read the current information, get stock quotations, click on links of interest.

Alternatively, if you want to put together your own portfolio to follow:

1. Under "My Places" on the right side of the "Welcome" window go to "Set My Places" and pick "My Portfolios" as one of the selected items from "Personal Finance."

2. Point the mouse cursor on "My Portfolios" and click.

3. In the new window "My Portfolios" (black letters on a multi-colored background), find the button that says "Create" on the lower left side of the window (see figure 11.11).

4. Point the cursor on this button and click.

5. In the new window (Step 1) fill in a name for your portfolio and press the "return" key.

6. In the next window (Step 2) fill in the information on your first position and, when you are done, click on "Add Item" in the center of the window (see figure 11.11).

A *Step-by-Step* Guide for Each Task

7. Repeat this to add additional positions.

8. Notice that you now have the name of each position on the right side of the window. When you are done adding positions, click on "Next."

9. Add cash or additional information as offered in "Step 3" and then click on "Finish."

10. You will now see the current information on each of the positions in your portfolio. Highlight an item and press "Details" to get all sorts of additional information. When you are done go to the small square on the top right of the window and click to close the window or press "Command" and the "W" key (⌘+W) simultaneously.

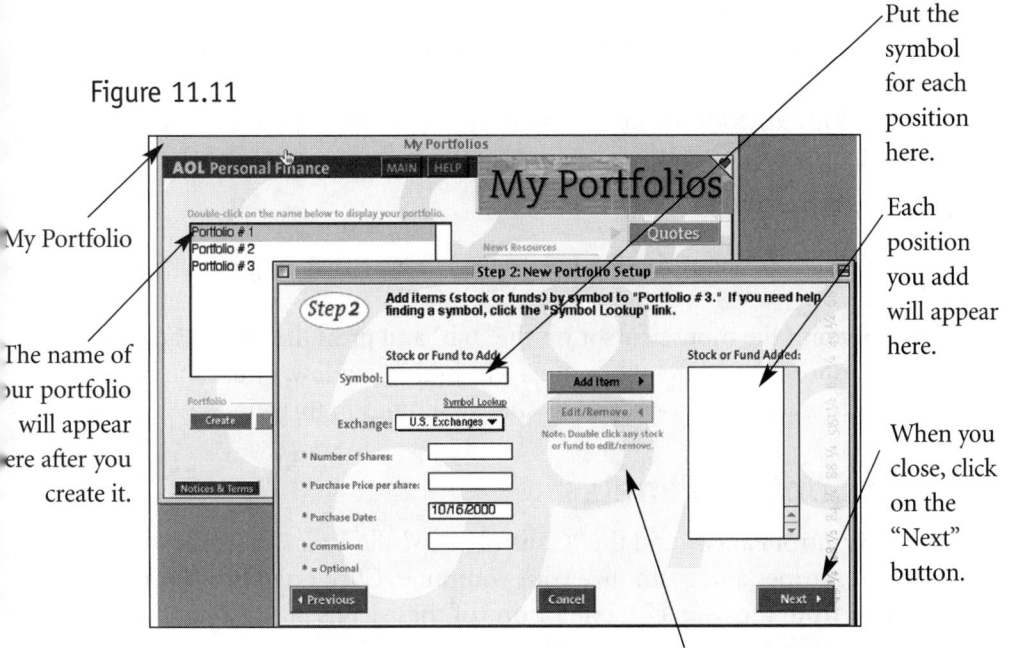

Figure 11.11

My Portfolio

The name of your portfolio will appear here after you create it.

Put the symbol for each position here.

Each position you add will appear here.

When you close, click on the "Next" button.

In "step 2" you can add positions to your portfolio by filling in the important information and clicking on the "Add Item" button.

135

The First Week with My New iMac

The Apple Menu

The "Apple" menu is the way to "get to" *everything* in your computer. It gives you access to programs and settings.

To Open this Menu

1. Point the mouse cursor on the "Apple" symbol on the extreme left side of the menu bar and press the mouse button once (click).

2. Use the mouse cursor to highlight the item that you are interested in and press the mouse button once (click).

3. Items like "Control Panels" or "Recent Documents" will have this symbol " ▶ "; this means more choices are available. When you highlight the main item you will see these other choices.

4. Move the mouse cursor up or down to highlight the program or item you want to open from "Control Panels" as an example.

5. Press the mouse button once (click) to open that program or item.

6. Point the mouse cursor on the "tab" and press the mouse button once to see different options within this window, or use the buttons, slides, arrows, etc., to change settings in this window.

The Control Panels

The "Control Panels" and the "Control Strip" allow you to change the default settings and customize your computer. Click on either "Control Panels" from the "Apple" menu or one of these icons on the "Control Strip" to adjust the features listed.

- Mouse: the speed, size, and appearance of the cursor.

A Step-by-Step Guide for Each Task

- Display: the look of the desktop and windows, screensavers, etc.

- Fonts: the size and appearance of the typeface.

- Sounds: the noises that the computer makes when it does certain tasks.

- Date and Time.

Shutting Down or Restarting Properly

1. Point the mouse cursor on the word "Special" on the menu bar at the top of your desktop and press the mouse button once (click).
2. Decide whether to "Shut Down" the computer, "Restart" it, or put it to "Sleep."
3. Point the mouse cursor on whichever command you want and press the mouse button once (click).
4. Wait for the machine to do what you have asked it to do.
5. If you shut the computer down completely, to restart it you will need to press the large button on the top right side of the keyboard with this symbol [⏻]. DO NOT DO THIS UNTIL THE COMPUTER HAS BEEN OFF FOR AT LEAST ONE MINUTE (union rules).
6. If you restart the computer, wait for it to start itself again. The screen will go black and then gray. It will show the usual "Welcome" window and items. This is "rebooting." Do not worry. When you see the desktop again you may use the machine.

Note: Usually one restarts the computer after loading a new program or changing a setting. Also, when nothing seems to work (like the mouse or the keyboard), restarting is quicker and easier than shutting down the computer and letting it rest for a minute before turning it back on.

The First Week with My New iMac

How to Set Up Folders

1. Point the cursor on the word "File" on the menu bar at the top of your desktop and press the mouse button once (click).

2. Point the mouse cursor on the word "New Folder" and press the mouse button once *or* press the "Command" key and the "N" key simultaneously (⌘+N).

3. Note that there is a new folder on the desktop titled "untitled folder."

4. Immediately start typing a name for this folder. (It is highlighted already; as you start typing, the name will go in the box below the folder. If it is no longer highlighted you must place the mouse cursor inside the rectangle, press the mouse button, and then type a name for your folder.)

5. You now have instant access to this folder because it is on your desktop.

6. Follow the same procedure to create folders inside of applications or within other folders (such as your document folder).

7. **Don't forget to name your folders.** If you have a general folder for documents, you might want additional folders for people, household activities, etc. (example: Correspondence, House, Car, Paul, Judith, Doctor-Lorraine, Lawyer-Neil, Travel, etc.).

8. To have instant access to folders created within other windows you must move the folder or item to the desktop. There are two ways to do this.

If you just want the folder on the desktop:

- Point the cursor on the folder you want to move.

- Hold down the mouse button.

A *Step-by-Step* Guide for Each Task

- Use the mouse to drag the folder to the side of the desktop.

- When the folder is on the desktop, release the mouse button.
or

If you want to make an "alias" or a shadow of the folder for the desktop while keeping the main folder in its original place:

- Point the cursor on the folder you want and highlight it by clicking once.
- Press the "Command" key and the "M" key (⌘+M) simultaneously and then release.

- The "alias" of the folder will be next to the original file and is distinguished from the original because it has an arrow in the lower left corner, and the name of the file is in italics followed by "alias" (see figure 11.12).

- Move this folder to the desktop by pointing the mouse cursor on the file, holding down the mouse button, dragging it to the

Figure 11.12

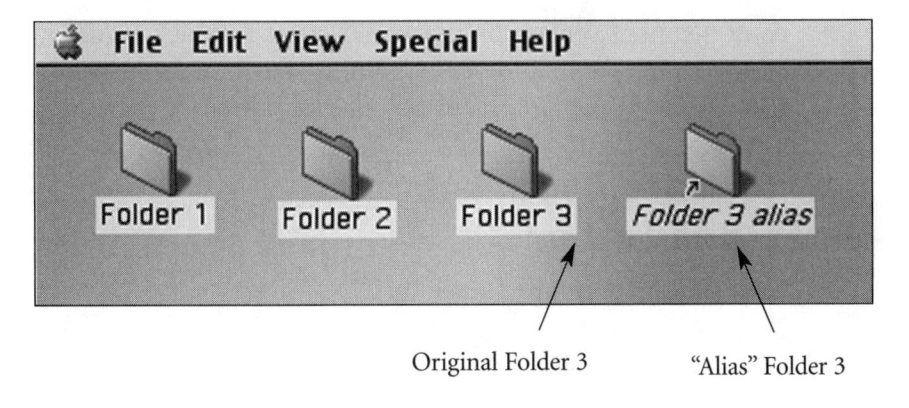

| File | Edit | View | Special | Help |

Folder 1   Folder 2   Folder 3   *Folder 3 alias*

Original Folder 3   "Alias" Folder 3

139

The First Week with My New iMac

desktop, and releasing the mouse button.

How to Move Folders and "Label" Folders
To Move a Folder

1. Open the window that contains the folder or file you want to move and then open the window into which you want the item to go.

2. Point the cursor on the item you want to move and hold down the mouse button.

3. Drag the folder to the window where you want the folder or file to go.

4. Everything will be moved to the new folder.

To Label a Folder

1. Point the mouse cursor on the folder to which you want to give a special color and press the mouse button once (click).

2. Point the mouse cursor on the word "File" on the menu bar and press the mouse button once (click).

3. Point the mouse cursor on the word "Label" and pick a color that you want for that folder by pointing the mouse cursor on it and pressing the mouse button once (clicking).

How to Write Documents, Notes, and Letters

1. Point the cursor on the "Macintosh HD" icon.

2. Press the mouse button twice (double-click).

3. Look at the window in front of you. Point the cursor on the folder that says "Applications" and press the mouse button twice (double-click).

A *Step-by-Step* Guide for Each Task

4. Point the cursor on the folder that says "AppleWorks 5" and press the mouse button twice (double-click).

5. Point the cursor on the "AppleWorks" icon and press the mouse button twice (double-click).

6. "**A** Word Processing" will be highlighted and you can then choose to "Create New Document" or "Use Assistant or Stationery" by pointing the mouse cursor at the button and clicking (see figure 11.13).

7. Then press the "return" key or point the mouse cursor on the word "OK" and press the mouse button once (click).

8. Press the "shift" key, the "Command" key, and the "S" key simultaneously (⇧+⌘+S) to show the "Save As" window (see figure 11.14).

9. Give your document a name in the lower box that is highlighted.

10. Decide if you want this document to go in this folder. If not:

    - Point the cursor on the top rectangle and move the arrows to pick a location. *or*

    - Look below at the various folders shown and point the cursor on the folder into which you want your document to go. Press the mouse button twice on that folder. *or*

    - Click on one of the buttons to the right for "New" or "Desktop."

    - Check that the correct folder name is shown in the box at the top of the window.

11. Point the cursor on "Save" and press the mouse button once (click) or press the "return" key.

The First Week with My New iMac

12. Type your document.

13. Make any changes you would like (see below).

14. Pause as you type to press the "Command" key and the "S" key (⌘+S) simultaneously about every five minutes.

15. When you are all done:

    - If you want to print your work press the "Command" key and the "P" key (⌘+P) simultaneously, decide exactly what you want printed, and press the "return" key. (See **How to Print Documents** on page 152.)

    - If you want to close the document, press the "Command" key and the "W" key simultaneously (⌘+W).

    - You will be asked if you want to "Save changes to the document." Point the cursor on the "Save" button and press the mouse button once (click) or press the "return" key.

Figure 11.13

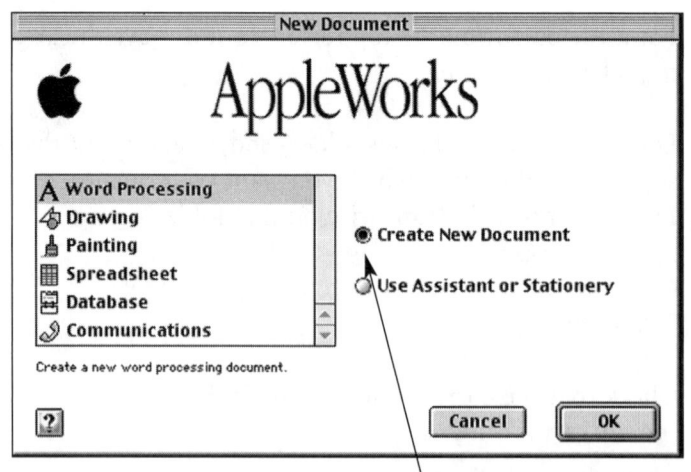

Create a new document by clicking on this button and then clicking "OK" or press the return key.

A *Step-by-Step* Guide for Each Task

Figure 11.14

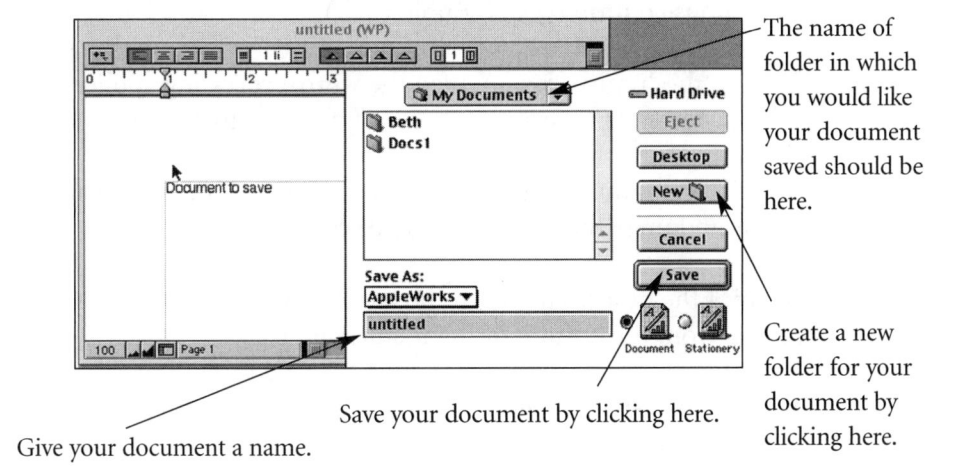

[Screenshot of Save dialog box with annotations:]
- The name of folder in which you would like your document saved should be here.
- Create a new folder for your document by clicking here.
- Save your document by clicking here.
- Give your document a name.
- Document to save

How to Make Templates

The purpose of a template is to have an original letterhead, fax form, or other item that you can open easily and that is customized. Each time you open it you are really getting a copy of your template with which to work. Therefore, you can write whatever you want and nothing happens to the original.

1. If you have made an "alias" of the AppleWorks icon and it is now on your desktop, double-click on this icon.

2. If you do not have this icon on your desktop:

    • Point the cursor on the "Macintosh HD" icon.

    • Press the mouse button twice (double-click).

    • Look at the window in front of you. Point the cursor on the folder that says "Applications" and press the mouse button twice (double-click).

    • Point the cursor on the folder that says "AppleWorks 5" and press the mouse button twice (double-click).

143

The First Week with My New iMac

- Point the cursor on the "AppleWorks" icon and press the mouse button twice (double-click).

3. Press the "return" key to open the word-processing application. You now have a plain piece of paper in front of you.

4. Point the mouse cursor on the word "Format" on the menu bar and press the mouse button once (click).

5. Point the mouse cursor on the term "Insert Header" (the second from the bottom of the menu) and click.

6. Fill in this space with the information you want to include, such as your name and address.

7. Highlight this information and then play with fonts, style, color, etc., to enhance your letterhead, newsletter, whatever.

8. When you are done point the mouse cursor on the word "File" on the menu bar, click once, highlight the term "Save As" and click once.

9. Notice that you can select either "Document" or "Stationery"—select "Stationery."

10. Point the mouse cursor on the button that says "Desktop" and click once.

11. Give your stationery or item a name (fill in the lowest rectangle in the window that is highlighted).

12. Press the "return" key or point the mouse cursor on the "Save" button and press the mouse button once (click).

Note: If you want to you can follow this same procedure to create a "plain piece of paper." Just leave the "header" blank and create a piece of "Stationery" as above. The advantage is that you will have something

A *Step-by-Step* Guide for Each Task

to work with that has more options than using "simple text" and will always be available on your desktop.

How to Save Documents

If you are saving a document for the first time, please read 8–11 in the previous section (**How to Write Documents, Notes, and Letters**).

Keyboard Commands

1. Type whatever you want.

2. Press the "Command" key and the "S" key at the same time (⌘+S).

Mouse Commands

1. Point the cursor on the icon that looks like a "folder with a downward pointing arrow" (on the button bar, eighth from the left under the word "Size") and press the mouse button once (click) (see figure 11.15).

Figure 11.15

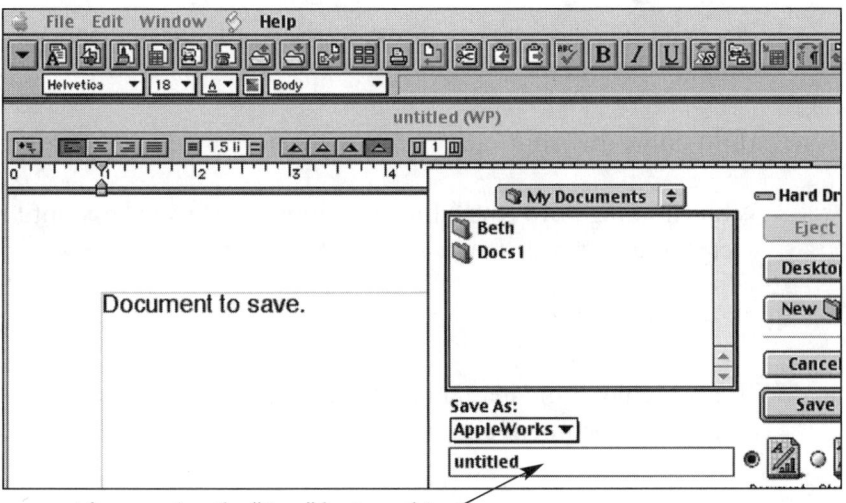

After pressing the "Save" button, this dialogue box will appear.

145

The First Week with My New iMac

How to Save Documents to a Folder of Choice Automatically

You can change settings so that whenever you want to save a document, a selected folder will appear as the default setting. To do this:

1. Point the mouse cursor at the "Apple" icon on the menu bar and click once.

2. Go to "Control Panels" and then "General Controls" on the submenu. Click once.

3. Look in the lower right section of the window at the word "Documents" and click on the button in front of "Documents folder" to make this your selection.

4. Close this window after making any other changes that appeal to you!

5. If you like, put the document folder on the desktop for easy access.

How to Highlight Something

1. Place the cursor at the beginning of the word, phrase, sentence, or paragraph.

2. Hold down the "shift" key.

3. While holding down the "shift" key, move the arrow keys until everything that you want is highlighted.

4. Release the "shift" key.

5. To un-highlight the item, place the mouse cursor on any open area of the document and press the mouse button once (click).

An Alternative Way to Highlight

1. Place the cursor at the beginning or end of item.

2. Hold down the mouse button.

3. While holding down the mouse button, drag the mouse to cover the entire area to be highlighted.

4. When the area is highlighted, release the mouse button.

Still One More Way to Highlight

1. If you want to highlight a whole word, place the cursor on the word and press the mouse button twice (double-click).

2. If you want to highlight a whole line, place the cursor on the line and press the mouse button three times (triple-click).

3. If you want to highlight the whole document, press the "Command" key and the "A" key at the same time (⌘+A).

Change the Look of Your Document: Formatting

First type your document. Then highlight the part you wish to change (see the previous section).

To Change the Style

Using Mouse Commands

1. Once an area is highlighted, point the cursor at the icon that will make the change you wish and press the mouse button once (click) (example: "**B**" to make bold or "U̲" to underline).

2. Point the cursor on any part of your document that is clear and press the mouse button to "un-highlight." *or*

The First Week with My New iMac

3. Highlight the area you want to change.

- Point the mouse cursor on the word "Style" on the menu bar.
- Highlight the style change you want.
- Press the mouse button once (click).
- Point the cursor on any part of your document that is clear, and press the mouse button once to "un-highlight."

Using Keyboard Commands

1. Highlight the area you want to change.

- Press the "Command" key and the "B" key (⌘+B) to make something bold.
- Press the "Command" key and the "I" key (⌘+I) to make something italic.
- Press the "Command" key and the "U" key (⌘+U) to underline something.

2. Point the cursor on any part of your document that is clear and press the mouse button once to "un-highlight."

To Change the Font You Are Using

1. Once an area is highlighted, point the cursor on the small, down arrow to the right of the name of the font (first white rectangle on the third bar from the top). Then press the mouse button once (click).

2. Point the cursor on the font you wish to use. Notice that the name of each font is actually written in the way that font looks.

A *Step-by-Step* Guide for Each Task

3. When the correct font is highlighted, press the mouse button once (click).

4. Point the cursor on any part of your document that is clear and press the mouse button once to "un-highlight." *or*

5. Highlight the area you want to change.

   - Point the mouse cursor on the word "Font" on the menu bar.

   - Press the mouse button once (click).

   - Highlight the font you want.

   - Press the mouse button once (click).

   - Point the cursor on any part of your document that is clear and press the mouse button once to "un-highlight."

To Change the Size of the Font

Using the Mouse

1. Once an area is highlighted, point the cursor on the white rectangle with a number (second from the left on the third bar from the top).

   - Point the cursor on the down arrow and press the mouse button once (click).

   - Point the cursor on the number of the size you wish to use and highlight it, then click.

   - Point the cursor on any part of your document that is clear and press on the left mouse button to "un-highlight." *or*

2. Highlight the area you want to change.

149

The First Week with My New iMac

- If you want to make the font larger, point the mouse cursor on the fourth icon from the right that shows an up arrow with the letter "A" and press the mouse button the number of times you need to get the correct size.

- If you want to make the font smaller, point the mouse cursor on the third icon from the right that shows a down arrow with the letter "A" and press the mouse button the number of times you need to get the correct size. *or*

3. Highlight the area you want to change.

- Point the mouse cursor on the word "Size" on the menu bar.

- Press the mouse button once (click).

- Highlight the size you want.

- Press the mouse button once (click).

4. Point the cursor on any part of your document that is clear and press the mouse button once to "un-highlight."

Using the Keyboard Commands

1. Highlight the area you want to change.

2. To pick a particular font size press the "shift" key, the "Command" key, and the "O" key at the same time (⇧+⌘+O) and then type the font size in the highlighted box.

3. To make the font one size smaller press the "shift" key, the "Command" key, and the "<" key simultaneously (⇧+⌘+<). Repeat to decrease the size.

4. To make the font one size larger press the "shift" key, the "Command" key, and the ">" key simultaneously (⇧+⌘+>). Repeat to increase the size.

A *Step-by-Step* Guide for Each Task

5. Point the cursor on any part of your document that is clear and press the mouse button once to "un-highlight" (see figure 11.16).

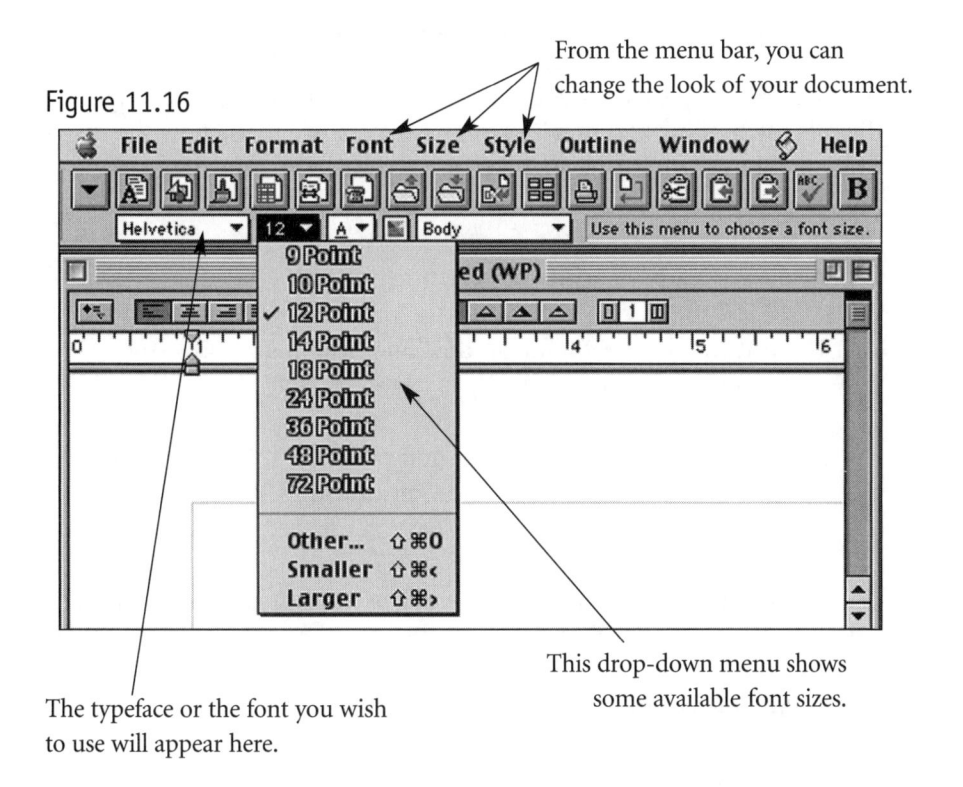

Figure 11.16

From the menu bar, you can change the look of your document.

This drop-down menu shows some available font sizes.

The typeface or the font you wish to use will appear here.

Note: You can perform a number of these tasks *at the same time* by leaving your word or paragraph highlighted while making numerous changes. Example: highlight a sentence and then change the size and style of the font, and underline it.

Also: If you *do not like* the changes you have made, highlight the words again and try something else or go back to the original by pressing "Undo Format" on the "Edit" menu or by pressing the "Command" key and the "Z" key at the same time (⌘+Z).

151

The First Week with My New iMac

How to Print Documents:
Preview

Before printing it is best to preview your document so that you can make any changes you would like. "Preview" includes a tool to enlarge the item, but AppleWorks does not allow you to really make changes directly. By looking at a preview you have a chance to see how the document will look on the page and check if your letter is centered, the paragraphs are spaced as you like, etc.

When you are ready to print your document:

1. Point the mouse cursor on the "File" menu and press the mouse button once (click).

2. Go down to the word "Print" and press the mouse button once, *or* press the "Command" key and the "P" key simultaneously (⌘+P).

3. Point the mouse cursor on "Preview" and press the mouse button once (click).

4. Preview your document.

5. Press the "return" key to close the preview. *or*

6. Point the mouse cursor on the icon that looks like a printer (11th from the left on the second line, under the word "Window") and press the mouse button once (click).

To Print Your Document

1. Point the mouse cursor on the word "File" on the menu bar, and press the mouse button once (click).

2. Point the mouse cursor on the word "Print" and click.

A *Step-by-Step* Guide for Each Task

3. A dialog box will open. It will:

- Confirm the printer you are using.

- Ask in what order you want the pages printed.

- Ask how many copies you want to print.

- Provide "Options" (for example, allowing you to print certain pages rather than the entire document).

4. When you have told the machine what you want, press the "return" key or point the cursor on the "OK" button and press the mouse button once (click) (see figure 11.17).

An Alternative Way to Print

1. Press the "Command" key and the "P" key (⌘+P) simultaneously, which is the key command to print.

2. Fill in the dialog box and/or just press the "return" key.

Figure 11.17

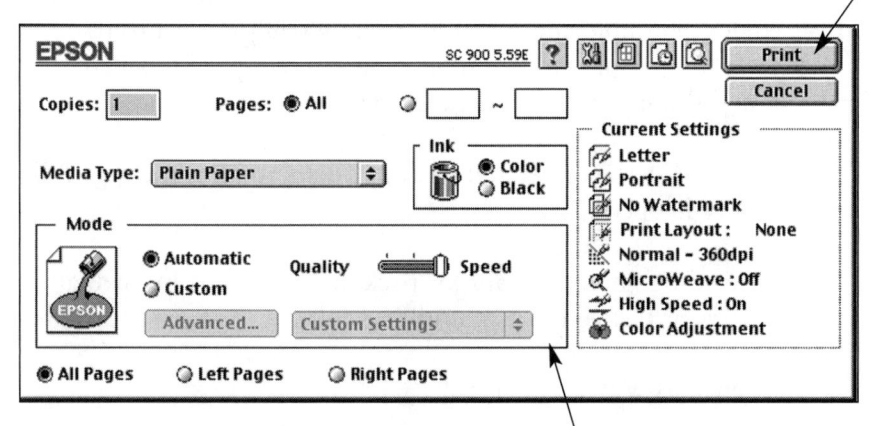

When you are ready to print, click on this button or press the return key.

Check all the information and make the changes you need such as number of copies, which pages, color or black and white.

153

The First Week with My New iMac

How to Back Up Files

It is important to back up (copy) your work onto a "disk" (floppy, zip, CD, etc.) so that you have an extra copy in the event that the computer really does "crash" and everything that is stored on your "hard drive" is lost. As an example I shall talk about a "floppy disk."

1. Insert a floppy disk into your disk drive.

2. Point the mouse cursor on the new icon (it looks like your disk and is now on your desktop) and double-click.

3. Point the cursor on the folder or file that you want to "back up"—it is either in a window or on your desktop.

4. Hold the mouse button down while you drag that folder to the icon for the floppy disk (looks like a disk and says "Mac Format").

5. Release the mouse button.

6. A box will appear that shows what is being transferred and how quickly it is being done.

7. Close the disk window when you are done or open the file or folder to double-check that everything really did get transferred. (Do not worry. You only made a "copy" of this item, you did not move it from its current position.)

If a file is too big to be copied onto a floppy disk, an error message will appear. If this happens:

1. Open the folder you want to "back up" and move individual folders or files to the disk until it is full.

2. Then start with another disk.

A *Step-by-Step* Guide for Each Task

Label everything immediately! Otherwise you will forget what you put on the disk.

How to Play the Card Game Solitaire

Point the cursor at the icon on the desktop that looks like a deck of cards and say, "Solitaire." (If the game is not on your desktop, see the instructions below.) Press the left mouse button twice (double-click).

For Directions on How to Play

1. Press the "Command" key and the "H" key (⌘+H) simultaneously.

2. Read the directions.

3. Press the "return" key.

To Play

1. Point the cursor on the card you want to move.

2. Hold down the mouse button and drag the card to the column where you want to place it.

3. Release the mouse button.

4. To turn cards in the deck, point the cursor on the deck of cards and press the mouse button once (click).

5. When you have run through the deck, point the cursor on the "Solitaire" icon where all the cards were initially and press the left mouse button once (click).

6. Start going through the deck again.

155

The First Week with My New iMac

To Play a New Game

    1. Press the "Command" key and the "N" key (⌘+N) simultaneously.

    2. A new game will be dealt.

To End the Game

    1. Press the "Command" key and the "Q" key (⌘+Q) simultaneously.

If Your Games Are Not on the Desktop

    1. Find the CD that says "iMac Software Install" and load it into the CD drive.

    2. Point the mouse cursor at the folder that says "CD Extras" and press the mouse button twice (double-click).

    3. Go to the "Eric's Solitaire Sampler" folder and double-click. (Eric is the guy who wrote this program.)

    4. Point the mouse cursor at the "sample" and hold down the mouse button while you drag this icon to the desktop.

    5. Your card game is now on the desktop ready to be opened whenever you want to play the game.

(Do you see why it is easier to have your games on the desktop?)

To remove the CD press the "Command" key and the "E" key simultaneously (⌘+E), or go to the word "Special" on the menu bar and click on the word "Eject" on the drop-down menu, or drag the CD icon to the Trash.

Other Games

Most card games are similar to solitaire, and by going to "Help" on the menu bar or looking through each of the options on other menus, you can

A *Step-by-Step* Guide for Each Task

get instructions on how to play each one of them. Some require "clicking and dragging"; some involve just pointing the cursor and clicking.

How to Listen to CDs and Use the Volume Control

Most computers today have speakers and CD drives. Yours is right in the front under the screen showing your desktop.

If you place an audio CD into your CD drive, it will start to play automatically. To control what you are listening to:

1. Point the mouse cursor at the "Audio CD" icon and press the mouse button twice (double-click).

2. Now point the mouse cursor at "Track 1" (or any track to which you would like to listen) and double-click.

3. A control panel will now appear and you can click on any of the buttons to change the settings just as you would on the CD player at home or in your car.

157

The First Week with My New iMac

Figure 11.18

Change the volume by pointing the mouse cursor on this tab, holding down the mouse button, and sliding the tab up or down.

To Change the Volume

1. Follow the three steps above.

2. Point the cursor on the volume control bar and hold down the mouse button while you drag the slide to the desired position (see figure 11.18).

3. Once you have the settings you like you can either move the control panel to a convenient location on your desktop or close it by pressing the "Command" key and the "W" key simultaneously (⌘+W).

How to Play a DVD Movie

1. Insert the DVD-CD into the CD drive on the front of your monitor.

2. Point the mouse cursor on the "Apple" menu and click.

3. Point the mouse cursor on the words "Apple DVD Player" and click once.

158

A *Step-by-Step* Guide for Each Task

4. Use the controller to start playing the movie, control sound, etc.

5. You can move the controller to another part of the screen or desktop by pointing the mouse cursor on the "Apple" symbol and holding down the mouse button while dragging the controller to a different location.

6. You can also hide the controller by going to "Windows" on the menu bar and clicking on "Hide Controller." Then you can use commands from the submenu under "Controls" on the menu bar.

7. The controller is really a lot of fun, so play with it and just click on everything you see.

How to Edit Your Own Digital Movies

1. First go to the "checker board" icon on the "Control Strip" and change the resolution of your monitor to at least 800 x 600.

2. Next point the mouse cursor on the "iMovie" icon that looks like a movie snapboard on the desktop and double-click.

3. Point the mouse cursor on the word "Help" on the menu bar and click to bring down the "Help" menu.

4. Point the cursor on "iMovie Tutorial" and press the mouse button once (click).

5. Read the instructions and follow the tutorial.

6. Now you are ready to work with your own movies.

The First Week with My New iMac

E-Books

In the early 1970s, courses in computer science became part of the required curriculum for a Masters of Science degree in Library Science. My classmates and I spent many hours debating the role of the traditional library once computers became smaller, cheaper, and easier to use. We discussed the ways computers could eliminate the need for a card catalogue, how libraries would communicate with each other in a matter of minutes rather than days, and how there would be large networks on which one could search for information on any topic. Some of us even thought that in the future, we would be able to put whole books on computers. Then a person could order books directly from the library or a publisher and read them from the machine without ever leaving their home.

The future is now. E-books (electronic books) are now available in a number of formats using a number of different software programs. At this time, the most accessible and versatile e-book program is provided by Microsoft and is called Microsoft Reader. As the publicity suggests, this is the next step for people who enjoy reading, but would like the advantages offered by the technology of the computer. These advantages include having any number of books stored on your computer as a personal library, getting almost any book that you would like "immediately" by downloading it, and being able to take your library wherever you go with your computer (or similar device). It also means that you can do things to your e-book that you can not or would not do to your traditional paper book.

The best features of an e-book include:

- The high resolution of the text and the ability to turn pages on the computer just as you turn pages on a traditional book.

- Changing the size of the font in order to make it easier to read.

A *Step-by-Step* Guide for Each Task

- Highlighting passages, making notations, and "book marking" important parts of the book.

- Looking up definitions of words that you do not understand.

- Searching for certain words or names in the book in order to find key information quickly.

- "Backlighting" your book to make it easier to read in dark conditions.

So what are the disadvantages? At the moment there is only one disadvantage and that is that the only software available for e-books is in the PC format. iMac users will have to wait a while until software is developed for this computer. Of course this does not mean that you need to sit and stare at an empty monitor. One of the reasons for telling you about e-books is to give you the latest information about new developments in the field. It is also to encourage you to practice the skills you will need to use this new technology. Some of the skills are basic like clicking and highlighting. Some of the skills are a bit more advanced such as searching for information on the Internet and then downloading it.

As practice, I would suggest that you go to the section in this book that tells you how to look up different topics on the Internet. Follow the instructions for signing on to AOL. Then when you see the AOL title bar, go to the line where it asks you to "Type Search words, Keywords or Web Address here" (third line from the top). Type in the address for the Microsoft Corporation. Wait for the "home page" to appear and then either type in the word "e-book" or "Microsoft Reader" in the search box on the left side of the page, point the mouse cursor on the word "Go" to the right, and press the left mouse button once (click). (Alternatively you can look down the topics in the center of the page and click on the "link" to the Microsoft Reader.)

The First Week with My New iMac

Now use the scroll bars to read all the information of interest to you on that page. In addition try pointing the mouse cursor at one of the "links" (the words in blue and underlined) to get additional information. Go ahead and play with this topic for a while. It will be interesting for you, and you will get to practice your skills in a fun and different way. When the software is available for the iMac, you will be ready to try it out right away!

A Appendices

The First Week with My New iMac

Appendix A
Troubleshooting and the Usual Questions, or, Why Won't This Stupid Thing Work?

I turned on the computer, but the screen is blank.
- Is the monitor getting any electricity? There should be a green light on the front of the monitor to show that it is on. If it is on then perhaps you need to adjust the brightness and contrast controls. This is just like the old-fashioned television! You will need to go to the "Control Panels" and then to the monitor to see if there is something that can be adjusted.
- If the screen is blank but the power button on the monitor is blinking with an amber light, then the machine is just "Sleeping." Press any key (**Note:** See last question in this Appendix) or click the mouse button to wake it up.
- Look in the owner's manual (the orange book) that came with your iMac. In the back are a few pages devoted to answering some basic questions.

I have asked the computer to perform a task and now I want to stop it. What do I do to get it to stop?
- To get the computer to stop what it is doing press the "Command" key and the "period" key (⌘+.) simultaneously.
- Another way to stop everything is to press and hold the "option" key and the "control" key and then press the "esc" key (option+control+esc).

All this information is very nice, but my computer does not seem to work like this at all! What is wrong?
- Is it possible that you are using a "PC" computer made by Dell, IBM, Gateway, Sony, etc., rather than an iMac made by Apple? If so, you are reading the wrong book. May I suggest that you buy my companion book, *The First Week with My New PC*, which should answer most of your questions.

Appendices

I double-clicked on a word by mistake and it was highlighted. What do I do?
- If you want to delete the word or change something about the way it looks, you have just stumbled onto something useful. If the cursor is on a word, you can highlight that word simply by double-clicking.
- If you did *not* want to highlight that word, then just move the cursor to some other area and press the mouse button once (click) to remove the highlight.

When something is highlighted, do I first have to delete these words before typing in the correction or change?
- No, that is one of the nice features of a computer as opposed to a typewriter. If something is highlighted, just start typing and the new words will appear in place of the highlighted words.

I "double-click" on an icon and nothing happens.
- Be sure you are really on the icon properly.
- If something is shaded it is "non-functioning." You will not be able to do that function so stop and think why the machine doesn't want to cooperate. Example: Perhaps you have asked it to send your e-mail now, but you are not "on-line" so it cannot do as you ask.

With programs and folders, how do I know when to press the mouse button once (click) and when to press it twice (double-click)?
- Good question! It varies, but usually pressing once will highlight or select something; pressing twice will open the program. Items on the desktop usually need two "clicks." Items in programs usually will open with one "click."
- If you are in "text" it is different. Pressing the mouse button once will place an "insertion point" at the spot where you want to do something. Pressing the mouse button twice (double-clicking) will highlight or select that word.
- I think it's a good idea to try one and then the other (just press the mouse button once and if it doesn't work press it twice—it can't hurt anything and it is easier to remember).

165

The First Week with My New iMac

- The key to mouse "clicking" is that you must click in the same spot each time. Also, if you want to "double-click" (press twice) you must do it quickly unless you have changed the mouse settings.
- If nothing happens in a short period of time, try again.

I do not remember what all the icons mean.
- You can change the settings so that if you point the cursor on an icon, a balloon will drop down and tell you what that icon does.

I do not remember what the word "icon" means!
- I should tell you to go to the Glossary, but just this once I will answer here. An "icon" is a picture used to show a certain job or task that can be performed.
- Example: If you click on the icon that looks like a printer, it sends the command to go ahead and print whatever document is currently open. The icon that looks like a check mark with "ABC" above it will check the spelling in your document if you click there.

When I am trying to work with the word-processing program in AppleWorks there are just too many icons, and I do not think I need to see all of them all the time. Can I get rid of some of them?
- Changing the way the icon or button bar looks is reasonable and easy. After all, why should you have to deal with this in the first week? When you have a word-processing window open in front of you, point the mouse cursor on the icon all the way on the left side of the bar—the one that looks like a down arrow.
- Press the mouse button once and notice that there is a check mark next to the "default" setting.
- Go down to "Edit Button Bar" and click.
- As you highlight each button or icon, a description of it appears. Just decide which ones you do not want to see and click on "Remove." When you are all done press the "return" key or click on "OK."

Appendices

What do all the icons on the desktop mean? When I point to them they don't provide any information.
- These icons represent programs and folders that you use a lot or that are permanently on your desktop thanks to the software manufacturers. They provide quick access to tasks you may want to do or folders that you work with all the time.
- Clicking on "Macintosh HD" is one way of seeing everything that is in your computer. It has an icon for each of the programs and folders in the computer. As you open one folder and then another, a new window appears. Think of it as peeling away the skin of an onion. Double-clicking on each folder will show you what is in that folder, and the next folder, and the next folder, right down to the files!
- You can put as many folders or programs as you wish on the desktop, but try not to get carried away. The idea is to make your life less, not more, complicated.
- Also note that one of the icons looks like a trash can. That is what it is. If you do not want something just point the cursor on that file or folder, hold down the mouse button and drag the item to the "Trash." Then release the mouse button to throw it away.

If I put something in the Trash is it really gone forever?
- RELAX! Nothing has been lost yet. Think of this as the beginning of the week and the trash is only picked up on Friday.
- Your document/file/folder will sit in the Trash until you "empty" it.
- To empty the Trash, point the cursor on the icon and press the mouse button twice (double-click). LOOK AT WHAT IS THERE. Do you really want to dump it? If the answer is yes, then go to "Special" on the menu bar and go down to "Empty Trash." Click on this command and then everything will be dumped. First, of course, there will be a dialog box checking to make sure you want to do this. If you want to dump everything then press the "return" key.

167

The First Week with My New iMac

How do I get something out of the Trash that I threw away by mistake?
- To get an item out of the Trash and back where it was originally just open the Trash and select (highlight) the icon or folder that you want to keep. Then press the "Command" key and the "Y" key (⌘+Y) simultaneously.

I think I have tried everything to get a CD to eject and nothing is happening. What do I do?
- Have you tried dragging the CD icon to the Trash, or pressing the "Command" key and the "E" key (⌘+E), or going to the word "Special" on the menu bar and clicking on "Eject"?
- If all of these failed, and only if these failed, take a paper clip and unbend it. Gently stick the end in the tiny hole just inside the right "bend" in the opening to the CD drive and press. This should solve the problem.

I put a DVD-CD into the CD drive and nothing is happening. How do I get it to play?
- This type of CD will not start automatically on the iMac. You need to go to the "Apple" menu and click on "Apple DVD Player." Then just play with the controls the way you would with the TV remote.

I try to do something and nothing happens except the computer making a "binging" sound.
- You have asked the computer to do something it cannot do.
- Perhaps you are trying to do something before you have answered one of the computer's "questions," or the command you are trying to give is currently shaded. Stop and think why the computer doesn't want to do what you are asking.
- See if there is a window that is asking you for some response and answer the question by pressing the "Y" (yes) or the "N" (no) key or pressing the "Enter" key to say "OK, that is fine."
- Perhaps you are not in an "active" window. If you try to give a command and the program is not active, the computer will "bing." Make sure the title bar (the top line) has dark letters and horizontal lines.

Appendices

How do I know when a program is "active"?
- You may see windows all over your desktop, but only one of them will have horizontal lines running along the top. This shows that this is the program that is open and "in use" or "active."

How do I get another program on the desktop to be "active"?
- All you need to do to activate a program is to "click" in any part of the window of a program that you see. Even if it is partially hidden, by clicking on anything, it will come to the front and be ready to use.
- Another way to find a "hidden" window is to look at the top right side of the menu bar. The name of the "active" window will be shown. If you want to see what else is open, point the mouse cursor on this space and click. All the other applications or programs will be shown. Click on the one with which you want to work.

How do I get the little balloons to appear to give me information about all these words and icons?
- To "turn on" this feature you need to point the mouse cursor on the word "Help" on the menu bar and press the mouse button once.
- Point the mouse cursor on the words "Show Balloons" to highlight them and click.
- Now you will see a balloon description of each item that you point to with the mouse cursor.

How do I get rid of these really annoying balloons that keep blocking my view of things on the desktop and distracting me?
- To "turn off" this feature you need to follow the instructions above, except now highlight and click on the words "Hide Balloons"!

The First Week with My New iMac

Even with the little balloons and icon names and menu information, I do not understand what all these words mean and what they do.
- Don't worry about most of the menu names and icons. The idea of this guide is a *basic* understanding of how to work the computer. If you are ready to delve into the intricacies of "Insert Footnote," "Outline," and "Publishing," you are ready to buy one of the more extensive computer guides.
- However, there is no reason why you cannot experiment. I suggest that you write a paragraph on any subject. Then try highlighting a line and pressing the icon that looks like a scissors on the line below the menu bar. The highlighted line is "cut out"! Next, point the cursor in the middle of some other line, click, and then go up to the icon line and click on the icon that looks like a clipboard. The line that you cut out should be there now.
- The idea is just to press different things and see what happens.

What do I do when I make a mistake and press the wrong key and half my letter disappears?
- Look on the icon or button bar (the second line at the top of your screen). The 12th icon from the left looks like a piece of paper with a "U turn" arrow. It will cancel or undo your last action. The first time you click on it the command will "Undo" what you've just done; the second time it will "Redo" your last action. (For fun, just click on each of these icons and watch your edit appear and disappear.)
- Alternatively, go to the "Edit" menu by pointing the cursor on the word "Edit" and clicking. Go to "Undo Format" and click. Or use the key command and press the "Command" key and the "Z" key (⌘+Z) to "Undo" the cut that you just made.
- To be on the safe side, it's best to click on the "Undo" icon or the words "Undo Format" from the "Edit" menu immediately after making a mistake. With some word-processing programs, if you wait and do even one thing, you cannot undo your previous mistake. Other programs let you undo a number of previous actions.

Why does everyone make such a fuss about "saving" things?
- Saving your work as you go along is a way of insuring that all your hard work is not lost. We have all forgotten to do this and "paid the price" by having hours of work disappear, forever. It is not fun when this happens! "Saving" can save you a lot of unhappiness.

I only wanted one word to be underlined/italicized/bold and now all the words that follow are like that. How do I get back to normal?
- You changed font and the computer did not know that you wanted to change only a portion of the text. When you have completed the section you are working on, you need to change back to the original font.
- Look at the icon or button bar and notice the "**B**" or "*I*" or "U." Before typing your next word or line, point the cursor on the appropriate letter and click. It is no longer active and everything will be normal.
- Another way to get everything back to normal is to look at the white rectangle all the way to the left on the third line. You should see the font that you want to see in the size that you would like. Change these settings if they are not as you wish.
- When all else fails, you can go to the "Edit" menu and click on "Undo Format" to undo what you have done. The key command for this is "Command" + "Z" (⌘+Z).

What do all the lines and numbers mean at the bottom of the window when I am writing something?
- These numbers tell you what page you are working on. You can also make the document larger or smaller by a "percentage" or by clicking on the icons to the right. This might make it easier to see.

How do I change the way the typing looks?
- To change the font you need to highlight the word/phrase/sentence you want to change and then use the tools on the icon or button bar to make changes. DO NOT FORGET: whatever you want to change must be highlighted.

The First Week with My New iMac

- If you change the look of a section and then decide you do not like it just remember "Undo Format" in the "Edit" menu.

I tried to give a new file a name and the machine made a noise and would not let me do it. What is the problem?
- The iMac will only allow you to use 31 characters and spaces. (This means that you can have a file name such as Lawyer-Jonathan-Wills & Trusts, but you cannot use the complete name of his law firm!)

Can I mix clicking the mouse button with using key commands?
- Yes. Sometimes it is easiest to point the cursor and click when you are using the mouse a lot. At the same time there is no reason you cannot use "Command" (⌘+C) to copy a highlighted area.

If I bought my own fancy mouse, why can't I use the right mouse button?
- BECAUSE I SAID SO! (I have been waiting for this question from you.) Actually, the right mouse button is very important and is a wonderful shortcut to all sorts of information. It will call up a menu with a set of actions from which to choose.
- IT IS ALSO SOMETHING YOU DO NOT NEED RIGHT NOW. It will only confuse you and you also might make some big mistakes that will delete or lose things in your computer.

All my friends have new multibutton mice like the PC mice. If I keep my original iMac "one button" mouse, will I feel deprived and develop "Mouse Envy"?
- You can get the same results with the one-button mouse as your friends do with their two-button mice by pressing the "control" key while clicking on something. A new set of options will appear just as if you had "right-clicked."
- However, if you are the type who loves new and interesting equipment then you probably will be envious of others and need a new mouse.

Appendices

How do I get rid of a window that I don't want to use?
- To get rid of a window:
  1. Point the cursor on the small box at the top left of your window and click on it with the mouse button. *or*
  2. Press the "Command" key + "W" key (⌘+W). *or*
  3. If you want to get rid of **all** the windows that you opened by accident when playing with different buttons, press the "option" key, the "Command" key, and the "W" key (option+⌘+W).
- However, if it is not a "window" but rather a dialog box, then you need to answer the question you are being asked before you can continue your work.

How do I get rid of the background desktop my child/friend added to my desktop?
- To change the "look" of your desktop you need to go to the "Control Panels" on the "Apple" menu, then highlight "Appearance" and click on it.
- Click on "Desktop." You now can make all sorts of changes.

How do I get rid of a child or grandchild (the one that is giving me more information than I can absorb)?
- I suppose the child is too old and too jaded to accept $1.00 to go out for ice cream?
- No, really. You have to be honest with the person. Tell him or her that you appreciate what you are being told, but you just are not following it right now. Suggest that it would be better to go over this when you are not so tired/hungry/preoccupied/overwhelmed.
- **This is important:** Do not have someone come to help you when you are not ready to listen and follow directions. It will make you unhappy and it will be very frustrating for the person trying to teach you. This is especially true when talking to your children on the telephone. I have a basic "three-strike rule." If we have tried to do something three times, unsuccessfully, it is time to stop! There is nothing wrong with saying, "Not now, thank you" or "This is not a good time" or "Let's try

173

The First Week with My New iMac

this again tomorrow." (I have said it to my mother and she has said it to me—and we are still talking to each other!)

Everything stopped working! I cannot get the mouse to move or any of the keys to work. What do I do?
- This happens to my mother all the time! The first thing to do is to check that the keyboard and the mouse are still plugged in. It is possible that if you have been sliding things around they have been disconnected. You need to make sure that the wires are pushed all the way in. Now try the mouse or control keys again.
- If that is not the problem, try pressing the "Command" key and the period key (⌘+.) simultaneously. Or you can try to force it to shut down by pressing the "option" key, the "Command" key and the "esc" key (option+⌘+esc) at the same time and then releasing them. (The latter is a "force quit," and you will need to respond to the dialog box that appears.)
- If this is not the problem then the easiest thing to do is to turn off the computer by pressing the "power" button on the keyboard. (Or if you have a "reset" button, press it once. Check your owner's manual for location.) WAIT ONE FULL MINUTE. Then press the power button again to restart the computer.
- The computer will go through all its start-up procedures and will probably tell you that it is unhappy that you shut it down improperly. It will tell you that it is checking everything to make sure it is OK. You will probably have to press the "return" key to start this process. Do this. Press the "return" key or click on the button. Then just wait and in a minute you will see the desktop again.

How do I know when to use the "Command" key, when to use the "shift" key, when to use the "control" key, or when to use the "option" key?
- The "Command" key can be used to issue direct commands without first going to a menu. For example, you can have the computer print your work by pressing the "Command" key

Appendices

and the "P" key (⌘+P). You did not have to go to the menu bar or the "Print" icon. If you do go to the menu bar you will see that this command is shown on the right side of the menu (next to "Print"). Another example is saving, which can be done by pressing the "Command" key and the "S" key (⌘+S) simultaneously.

- Other modifier keys are used for more advanced actions or the actions that are not used as frequently. The menus will show many of these options, so it is easy to learn the ones you want to use.
- **Important:** Remember to press the modifier keys in the order shown either in written directions or from the menus and then press the appropriate letter key. Remember to hold down keys until the action is done and then release.

Why should I be interested in going to some of the Web sites you mention?

- I have given a number of interesting Internet addresses to help start you out. I have tried most of these myself and thought they were either informational or funny.
- I also think that by trying some of these sites, you will understand the breadth and depth of the Internet and become aware of many things you did not realize were available.
- For an example, I suggest going to the National Public Radio Web site, www.npr.org.
  1. When you get to the home page, go down to radio shows and select *All Things Considered.*
  2. If you want to see what is on today, that is fine. If not, click on "Archives" and pick one of last week's programs.
  3. Scroll through the list of reports for the day and notice that they also show what musical selections were played.
  4. Pick one of the reports and click on the "link" (the blue words).
  5. Now wait. In a moment another window will open and you will actually hear the report that was broadcast over the air! You never have to worry about missing an item on this show!

The First Week with My New iMac

- What I have suggested for National Public Radio can also be done for other radio stations and several television news networks. Just try it for fun!

How do I program my VCR so that the clock stops blinking at me?
- For that answer you will need to buy my next book: *My VCR, My Friend*.

If I am asking all these questions, should I consider moving on to a more advanced instruction book?
- Sure, why not? After all, this is a very basic guide. Now that you know how to get everything "up and running," you will feel a lot more comfortable following some of the other computer books. It will also be easier to think of your question and find an answer using another book's index. Enjoy!

To wrap things up, I would like to make a point about asking questions and calling Technical Support telephone numbers for help. The number one question people ask when they call the technical support line at one of the largest computer companies in the world is:

Where is the "Any" key? I cannot find it on the keyboard!
- This question arises from a prompt that is still part of some older programs on other computers in which a person is asked to "Press any key to continue." I am not making this up. People actually do ask the tech support people to tell them where this key is on their keyboard. The company is rewriting its software to say, "Press the 'Enter' or 'return' key." So you see, you really should not worry about asking a stupid question. Most of them have already been asked.

Appendix B
Some Important Key Commands
Basic Functions

The "Command" key is the key with one or both of these symbols on it: ⌘ and/or . To use the key commands below first press and hold the "Command" key and then press the key (or keys) specified. Then release all the keys.

Close Window	"Command" + "W"
Close All Windows	"Command" + "option" + "W"
Copy	"Command" + "C"
Cut	"Command" + "X"
Duplicate	"Command" + "D"
Eject (CD)	"Command" + "E"
Eject floppy disk	"Command" + "shift" + "1"
Find	"Command" + "F"
Get Information	"Command" + "I"
Help	"Command" + "?"
Make Alias	"Command" + "M"
New Folder or Document	"Command" + "N"
Open	"Command" + "O"
Paste	"Command" + "V"
Print	"Command" + "P"
Put Away	"Command" + "Y"
Quit	"Command" + "Q"
Save	"Command" + "S"
Save As	"shift" + "control" + "S"
Select All (highlight everything—whole document, all the icons in a file, etc.)	"Command" + "A"
Trash—move something to can	"Command" + "delete"
Undo	"Command" + "Z"

The First Week with My New iMac

When in Word Processing, in Order to Format:
Highlight the text, then:
Bold   "Command" + "B"
Italics   "Command" + "I"
Plain Text   "Command" + "T"
Underline   "Command" + "U"

E-mail
To write mail (America Online)   "Command" + "M"

Appendices

Appendix C
Some "World Wide Web" Addresses of Interest

Please note: I neither endorse nor suggest that you use any of these addresses. They are included as a "starting" point to help get you involved with the Internet and to show you how logical the "addresses" are. Many popular magazines, newspapers, and television shows announce new and interesting sites all the time. Be prepared to copy down anything that sounds interesting to you.

Search Engines

Altavista	www.altavista.com
Ask Jeeves	www.askjeeves.com
Excite	www.excite.com
Fast	www.alltheweb.com
Google	www.google.com
Northernlight	www.northernlight.com
Snap	www.snap.com
Yahoo	www.yahoo.com

Search Engines' Search Engine

This uses all the search engines	www.webferret.com

General Information

Weather
The Weather Channel	www.weather.com
National Weather Service	www.noaa.gov

News
Newsweek Magazine	www.newsweek.com
Time Magazine	www.time.com
CNN	www.cnn.com

The First Week with My New iMac

CNN Video Select
  (video news clips)   www.cnn.com/videoselect
MSNBC (cable TV station)   www.msnbc.com
National Public Radio   www.npr.org
British Broadcasting Company   www.bbc.co.uk

Education
Smithsonian Institution (museums) www.si.edu
Library of Congress (everything) http://lcweb.loc.gov/library/
New York Public Library
  (almost everything)   www.nypl.org
Encyclopaedia Britannica (charge) www.eb.com
The Encyclopedia Mythica
  (mythology)   www.pantheon.org/mythica
Language   www.wordsmith.org
American Sign Language   www.hoh.org/~mastertech/
                                  asldict.spml

Services
Postage and Zip codes   www.usps.gov
Postage   www.stamps.com
Finding people   www.switchboard.com

Health

Directories
U.S. Dept. of Health and
  Human Services   www.healthfinder.com
National Library of Medicine
  (NIH)/Medlineplus   www.nlm.nih.gov/medlineplus
Mayo Clinic   www.mayohealth.org

Organizations
American Heart Association   www.americanheart.org
American Diabetes Association www.diabetes.org
American Association
  of Retired People   www.aarp.org

Linking Human Systems
(physical, mental, and addictions)   www.linkinghumansystems.com

Nutrition and Food
Tufts University   www.navigator.tufts.edu
Internet Chef (30,000 recipes)   www.ichef.com/ichef-recipes/
Recipes   www.epicurious.com
Groceries (for home delivery)   www.yourgrocer.com
                                     www.peapod.com
                                     www.webvan.com
Wine (for home delivery)   www.wine.com

Alternative Medicine   www.altmedicine.com

Pharmacy   www.drugstore.com

Fitness Link   www.fitnesslink.com

Travel

Tickets, etc.
Travel information   www.travelocity.com
Travel and more   www.priceline.com
Travel and tickets   www.expedia.com
More ideas   www.smarterliving.com

Maps
Maps and driving instructions   www.mapblast.com
Another map service   www.expediamaps.com
Still one more   www.mapquest.com

Restaurants
Fodor's restaurant index   www.fodors.com
Zagat's   www.zagat.com

The First Week with My New iMac

Entertainment

Movies
Internet Movie Database	www.imdb.com
Reviews	www.moviefone.com
Rent DVD movies	www.kozmo.com
	www.urbanfetch.com
	www.netflex.com

Books
Barnes & Noble	www.bn.com
Amazon	www.amazon.com
More books	www.bookfinder.com
Book news, reviews, etc.	www.bookwire.com
Comparison of prices	www.bestbookbuys.com

Music
Directory	www.listen.com
General	www.mp3.com
Lyrics	www.lyrics.ch/index.htm
Software	www.real.com

Sports
General	www.sportsline.com
General	www.espn.com
Statistics	www.rotonews.com

Shopping, Games, and Toys
Connection to many stores	www.shopnow.com
Comprehensive shopping resource	www.buy.com
Connection to buy gift certificates	www.giftcertificates.com
Toy shopping	www.etoys.com
Chocolate in every way	www.chocolatepicture.com
Auctions	www.ebay.com
More auctions	www.artnet.com
Download software	www.shareware.com
More software	www.download.com

Appendices

Games   http://games.yahoo.com
Shopping search engine   www.piig.com
This site is a different approach to finding things on the Web. Type in www.p(whatever you are interested in)g.com (example: www.pbooksg.com) and it will take you directly to on-line stores in your area of interest.)

Important: If you are buying something on the Internet there are four things to remember:
1. Make sure it is a "Secure Site," which means there should be a little icon visible that looks like a closed padlock.
2. Always pay by credit card so you will only be liable for a maximum of $50 if something goes wrong.
3. Only give your credit card number and billing/shipping address—*no personal information* that is not required.
4. Ask about the site's return policy.

Finance

General Information
Wall Street Journal   www.wsj.com
More information   www.thestreet.com
Still another site   www.fool.com

Taxes
Advice   www.taxprofet.com
Planning   www.irs.ustreas.gov
More advice   www.fairmark.com

Computer Information

MacAddict   www.macaddict.com
Macworld   www.macworld.com
Mac Today   www.mactoday.com
Tips and info   www.gilesrd.com/
Apple Web site   www.apple.com

183

The First Week with My New iMac

General information
  on everything!   www.cnet.com
Shopping   www.onsale.com
More shopping   www.edw.com

Unusual and Interesting

Blue Mountain   www.bluemountain.com
   Free electronic greeting cards for every occasion and in several languages. A great way to send some cheer.

United Nations World Food Program   www.hungersite.com
   A way to give food to a starving person at no cost to yourself. Each log-on provides a single serving of food; one log-on a day is permitted. "Bookmark" this site. Make a difference!

Kooponz.com   www.kooponz.com
   Money-saving coupons for you to print and clip—good in 44 states.

Another site for money-saving coupons   www.coolsavings.com

Outletzoo   www.outletzoo.com
   Clearance shopping site where prices drop as time goes on!

Cartoons   toon@cartoonbank.com
   A plethora of laughter from the *New Yorker* magazine

Duct Tape   www.octane.com/ducttape.html
   Everything you want to know!

A World of Tea   www.stashtea.com
   History and more

Appendices

Birds   www.birder.com
    A megasite for bird-watchers

SETI (Search for   www.setiathome.ssl.berkeley.edu
    Extraterrestrial Intelligence)
    A way to help scientists and a great screen-saver

Appendix D
E-mail Etiquette: "Smileys," Abbreviations, and Other Tips

You may or may not have heard the term "shouting." It refers to a message sent in ALL CAPITAL LETTERS. This is very annoying. It is also difficult to read. *Do not* type your messages using all capital letters because it is considered rude!

You may have heard the term "flaming." To "flame" someone is to send an insulting or angry message. This is also considered rude. If you are really that angry with someone you know, then call the person on the telephone and straighten it out. If you do not know the person to whom you are sending angry messages over the Internet, why are you getting so upset with a stranger?

"Smileys" (also called "emoticons") are a combination of keyboard characters that express a feeling. They use colons, semicolons, apostrophes, dashes, parentheses, and letters to make (sideways) "faces." (When you try to type some of these symbols into a Word document, the program will automatically change the characters to a graphic symbol, but in an e-mail message the characters stay as they are typed.) Some people like to include them in their messages, so here are some examples.

Smile	:-)
Frown	:-(
Indifferent	:-I
Cry	:'-(
Wink	;-)
Laugh	:-D
Kiss	;-x
Shocked	:-o
Screaming	:-@
Angry	>:|

Appendices

E-mail abbreviations are a type of shorthand using the first letter of each word in a phrase to convey a thought. It saves time typing out these phrases, and many people already use the abbreviations in everyday speech. An example is saying "ASAP" rather than "As Soon As Possible." Other examples include:

FYI	For Your Information
LOL	Laugh Out Loud
IRL	In Real Life
B4N	Bye for Now
F2F	Face to Face
CUL8R	See You Later
ROTFL	Rolling On the Floor Laughing
IMO	In My Opinion
IMHO	In My Humble Opinion (rarely meant that way!)
IOW	In Other Words
BTW	By the Way
WRT	With Respect To
FAQ	Frequently Asked Question
RSN	Real Soon Now
GMTA	Great Minds Think Alike
TIA	Thanks in Advance
BRB	Be Right Back
AWTTW	A Word to the Wise
PD	Public Domain
RL	Real Life

Appendix E
Tech Support:
Phone Numbers and Web Site Addresses

While this is a very useful guide in many ways, the fact is that everyone needs to call Tech Support for help every now and then. Do not be afraid to do this. The people at the other end of the phone are wonderful and patient. They also want to be helpful. Just recognize that you may have to wait *a very long time* to get someone on the line to help you. For this reason you should have food, drink, and a book or project to work on within reach before placing the telephone call.

Apple Computer Company

For help with the computer itself start here:
 1-800-SOS-APPL
 (1-800-767-2775)   www.apple.com

Software Companies

Adobe	1-408-536-6000	www.adobe.com
Corel	1-800-772-6735	www.corel.com
FileMaker Corp.	1-415-382-4700	www.filemaker.com
Intuit	1-650-944-6000	www.intuit.com
Lotus	1-978-988-2500	www.lotus.com
Microsoft	1-425-882-8080	www.microsoft.com
Symantec–Norton	1-800-441-7234	www.symantec.com

Appendices

Appendix F
Healthy Computer Habits: Taking Care of Yourself Physically and Mentally

As I mentioned before, it is very easy to become enamored of your computer. Before you know it you have spent a whole evening "surfing the Web" or playing games. Perhaps you are enjoying the Word program so much that you are writing your own book! You may be familiar with terms like "ergonomics," "carpal tunnel syndrome," and "Internet addiction." However, you see no reason why any of this would apply to you—after all, you are just a beginner and not really "working" at the computer. If you believe this, you are *wrong*! On a serious note, I strongly urge you to read the section below and follow the advice given.

Your Physical Well-being

While we have discussed "setting up" your computer, we have not discussed how you should position yourself in front of the computer. This gets into ergonomics, the science concerned with the safe and efficient interaction of people and machines. Here are some things you need to check and do so that you sit comfortably and do not injure yourself while using the computer.

Position

- You must sit squarely in front of the keyboard and monitor—not at an angle (see diagram on page 191).

- The keyboard should be at a height that allows your elbows to bend at a 90-degree angle. You do not want to have "cocked" wrists (see diagram).

- Position yourself in the chair so that when you look straight ahead at your monitor, your eyes are focused on the center of the screen (see diagrams).

189

The First Week with My New iMac

- You should have your chair at a height that allows your feet to rest on the floor (use a little footstool if necessary—the best type is sloped).
- Try not to lean forward with your chin pushing out (see diagrams—good position and bad position).
- Make sure your keyboard is comfortable for you. There are several styles, and another one might "fit" your hands or size better than the one you have.
- There are several types of "mice" as well. Go to a computer store and test a few to see if there is one that's easier for you to use.

Exercises

Every 20 minutes STOP WHAT YOU ARE DOING! It is very important to get up and move around a bit.

- Place your two hands together with the palms touching and the fingers pointed up. Now slide your hands down, holding the palms together so that you feel the stretch in your wrists (see diagram).
- Roll your wrists in a circular motion. (Yes, both directions—let's stay balanced!)
- Place your left wrist on your right forearm and press down with the wrist while pressing up with your arm. Now put your right wrist on your left forearm and do the same thing (see diagram).
- Drop your head down a bit and let your chin tuck back toward your neck. Now place your fingers on your chin and gently press your chin back with your fingers while you push your chin forward (see diagram).
- While sitting in a chair, raise your legs off the floor so that your feet are not touching the ground. Now rotate your ankles in such a way that it is as if you are using your feet to "write" the alphabet. Go through the whole alphabet twice. (This exercise is not really that important for your work on the computer, but it is a great exercise to keep your ankles strong, and it is easy to do anywhere!)
- Go get a drink of water. You need eight glasses a day anyway, and it will clear your head for the work you are doing.

Appendices

Diagram A.1

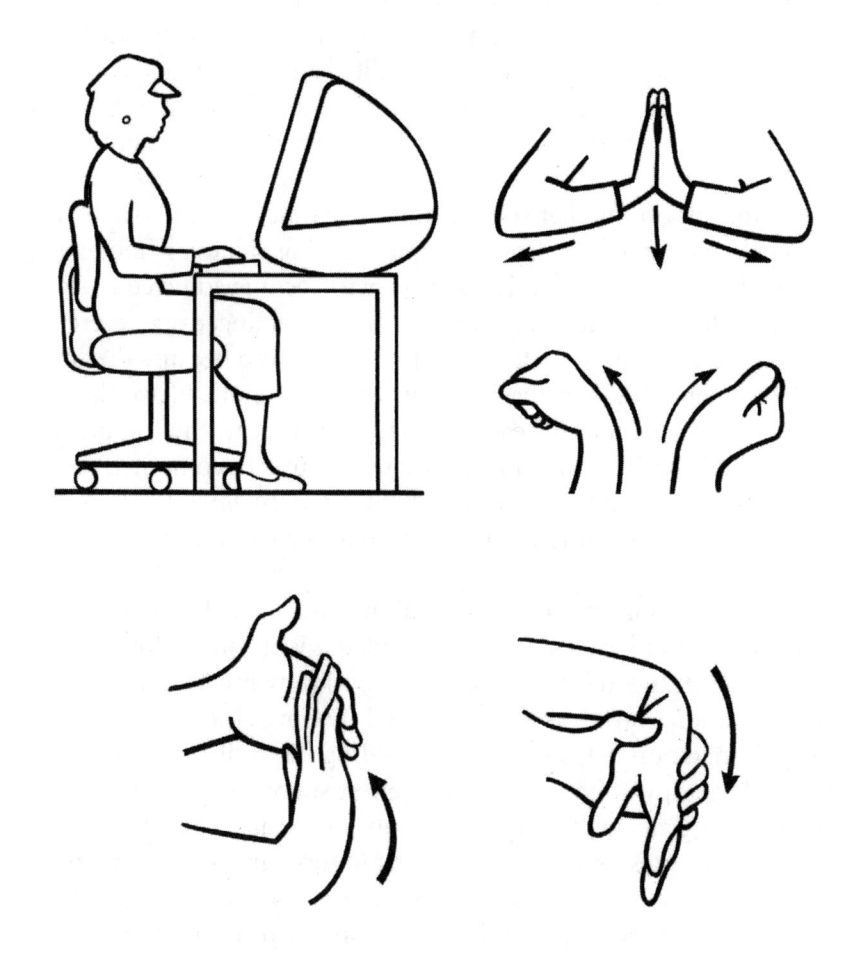

For Those Who Wear Bifocals
It is important to understand that the computer screen is a new and interesting distance from your face. You are looking at a machine that is farther away than a book, but closer than a television. Go to your eye doctor and explain that you are now using a computer. He or she will make a lens the right focal distance and similar to the reading portion of your bifocals. This means you will not have to tilt your head back, injuring your neck, to use the tiny reading circle on standard bifocals.

The First Week with My New iMac

Your Mental Well-being
Earlier in the book, I made a joke about naming your computer. I suggested that giving the machine a "name" would personify it and cause you to spend more time with it. The reality is that for some people, spending time on the computer does become an obsession. It has been recognized by authorities and given a name: Internet addiction.

Again, you may think that you are only a beginner and can barely "sign on" let alone spend your days and nights playing games or "looking up things." The reality is that it is just as easy to become addicted to this form of entertainment as any other, such as gambling, drugs, exercise, sex, etc. Many people literally forget to eat and sleep because they are totally immersed in their machine. On a personal note, I have already told you that I spent hours each night trying to "beat" the computer at solitaire while visiting my mother and setting up her computer. When I start a writing project, it is very difficult for me to remember to pick up my son at school or to even stop to go to the bathroom!

It is for this reason that I warn you about this issue. It is a serious problem for many people. I have included a Web site address that will be useful to you if you or anyone you know might have a problem with addictions. It is a group called Linking Human Systems™. This organization helps families by guiding them through intervention and therapy. It has one of the highest success rates in the country in helping all ages and types of "substance" abusers get the help they need. It is also a resource for consultation and counseling on health issues, both mental and physical. If you have any concerns about your own behavior or that of anyone in your family, you might want to go "on-line" and see what the organization can do for you (www.linkinghumansystems.com).

Glossary

The First Week with My New iMac

This glossary includes more words and terms than you would normally expect in a book on basic computers. In fact, there are some words that you will not find in the body of this book. I chose to include additional information because you might be reading articles or hearing terms that you do not understand. My thought is that this glossary can be a resource to you well past the first week.

Access time The amount of time it takes for data to arrive at a particular place after it has been requested.

Active desktop A feature of Windows 98® that allows you to view Web pages and mini-programs directly on your desktop. Mini-programs include such things as a stock ticker, a weather map, and a clock.

Active window The window that is currently in use on your desktop, and the window that contains the cursor. You can recognize it by the title bar, which is a horizontal blue bar at the top of the window with white letters describing the window. (If the window is not active, then the bar is light gray with dark gray letters.) Only one window can be active at a time.

Address The exact location on a disk where information (a file) is stored. Addresses are used to find files on your computer and on the Internet. (On the Internet, addresses are also called URLs.)

Alias A file or folder that represents another one that is exactly the same, but is stored in another part of the computer. If you double-click on an alias it will open the file, folder, or application just as if you had selected the original. Often an alias of a file will be placed on the desktop for easy access. You can recognize it because the name is always in italics and there is a small arrow on the lower left corner of the icon.

Apple menu A menu that is symbolized by the multicolored Apple logo and is found on the far left side of the menu bar at the top of the desktop. It is the way to access many programs on the computer, but more important, it is the way to access the Control Panels, Recent Documents you have been working on, etc.

Glossary

AppleWorks® A program that is a combination of word processing, drawing, painting, spreadsheet, and data gathering. As an example, it is the program that you use to write letters and documents.

Application Another word for program. It is software that does a particular task.

Arrow 1) An icon that appears on the desktop and is controlled by, and shows where, the mouse is moving. 2) Keys on the keyboard that look like arrows and move the cursor (or insertion point) one place at a time in the direction indicated.

ASCII The acronym for "American Standard Code for Information Interchange" (pronounced "askee"). This is the standard code system that allows different computers to "talk" to each other by assigning numeric values to every letter, number, symbol, etc.

Backup A copy of data files or programs that you create as insurance in case there is an accident and your original is damaged or lost.

Bit The basic or smallest unit of measurement for electronic data. It is a contraction of BInary digiT, and it stands for 0 (on) or 1 (off). When eight bits are combined it makes a unit called a "byte." Computers can combine "0"s and "1"s to represent every letter, number, and punctuation mark.

Boot To start the computer. The computer uses information that it has stored in its own section of the hard drive to "restart" itself. It then loads the rest of the operating system into memory. The term comes from the idea that the computer is "pulling itself up by its own bootstraps."

Bounce A term used when e-mail is returned to the original sender because it could not be delivered due to an error. For example, if a message is undeliverable because of an incorrect address.

The First Week with My New iMac

Browser A program that gives you access to the Internet and helps you to retrieve information easily from the World Wide Web.

Bug An error in the hardware or software of the computer. If it is in the software, changes must be made to the program. If it is in the hardware, then it is a real mess, as new circuits must be made and installed.

Button An element that is part of a GUI (see *Graphical User Interface*) and lets you select an option from a dialog box, a bar, etc.

Button bar The horizontal bar of buttons or icons that is just below the menu bar. These are command buttons, and each icon represents the most frequently used tasks. For some people, it is easier to point the cursor on one of these icons and click than to use a pull-down menu or key command.

Byte The amount of space needed to represent a single character (eight bits). This is a very small unit and many bytes are needed to handle a word-processing program, so terms for larger units have developed, such as "kilobyte," "megabyte," and "gigabyte" (1 billion bytes).

Cache A folder for temporarily storing frequently used files in a special area on your computer. In effect, it speeds up the operation of the computer for those tasks performed most often.

"Cancel" button An element in a dialog box, that is a GUI (See *Graphical User Interface*). Pressing this button allows you to cancel an operation or move to the next higher level of a program. You can easily "cancel" an action either by clicking on this button or by pressing the "esc" key (the escape key).

Carpal tunnel syndrome A form of wrist and hand injury caused by repetitive movements such as typing. It is important to have an ergonomic position while seated at the computer, and to take frequent breaks while typing to avoid this problem.

CD-ROM An acronym for "compact disk read-only memory." A CD-

Glossary

ROM is a high-capacity storage device that can hold up to 650 megabytes of data, which is the equivalent of the information on 500 floppy disks or 300,000 pages of text. The information on the disk is permanent and cannot be changed.

CD-ROM drive A special computer disk drive that reads CDs. On the iMac this drive is internal and is placed right under the monitor screen.

Check boxes These are square boxes within dialog boxes that allow you to select or deselect your choices by clicking (or toggling on and off). The selection is "on" when a check mark appears. Often you can select more than one option.

Chip An integrated circuit.

Circuit board The board on which chips are mounted. The main circuit board of a computer is often referred to as the "motherboard."

Click To press and release a mouse button quickly to make a selection. If you have a mouse with several buttons, it usually refers to pressing the left mouse button once.

Clipboard The place where information is temporarily held after it has been copied or clipped from a document. This information can then be transferred to another location.

Close box The button you use to close a window. It is the small square on the top left side of a window along the title bar.

Closing a window This means that you are removing the contents of a window from memory and from the screen. It is important to "save" your work, otherwise all the data will be lost when you close the window. If you close an application window it means you have stopped working in that program.

Collapse box The button that causes a window to "shrink" so that all that is seen is the title bar. This creates more room to work on the

The First Week with My New iMac

desktop while keeping windows visible. It is the small square on the extreme right of the title bar.

Command key This key is found to the left and right of the space bar and has both the Apple logo and the command symbol. It is used with other keys to do various tasks when you do not want to use the mouse.

Control key A key that is found on the lowest row of the keyboard on the extreme left side. It is used in combination with other keys as a shortcut to tell the computer to do various tasks.

Control Panels A folder in "System Folder" on the hard drive that shows hardware applications and allows you to change the settings and options for both hardware and software, thus adjusting many system features.

Control Strip A group of small icons that are at the bottom of the desktop along a gray bar. They can be used as shortcuts to change many of the settings that are found in the Control Panels folder. The strip can be retracted so that it takes up minimal space on the desktop and extended when you want to adjust things more often.

CPU An acronym for "Central Processing Unit." This controls the computer and handles the main processing. It is commonly referred to as a "chip."

Crash An unexpected stoppage while working on some task or program. The computer does not respond to any key or mouse commands. It is caused by a failure or error of either the software or hardware. A computer virus can also cause a crash. If this occurs, you will probably have to "restart" (reboot) your computer. If you have not backed up or saved your work, it might be lost in a system crash.

Cursor A special character on the desktop or in an application that shows where the next character will appear when something is typed. It can be controlled or moved by using the arrow keys on the keyboard

Glossary

or by moving the mouse to the desired spot and clicking. The cursor changes shape as it moves around the screen, indicating when it can perform different tasks. (When working with text it is also called the "insertion point" and it blinks.)

Cursor keys (See *Arrow 2.*)

Data Information in a form that the computer can use for processing.

Database Any collection of related information or "objects" (reports, forms, tables, etc.) created, organized, and controlled by a database management system.

Data file A file containing information.

Default The standard or predefined setting. It is used if you specify no other setting.

Delete To get rid of something. When you delete a folder it goes to the "Trash" and it stays there until it is purged or restored.

"delete" key A key on the upper right side of the keyboard that moves the cursor one space to the left. As it does this, it erases one character at a time. (Note that to the right of the basic keyboard there is another "delete" key that has "del and a forward arrow" as its symbol. This key will delete letters to the right of the blinking cursor.)

Desktop An on-screen version of a desktop that shows windows, icons, files, and accessories that you use to do your work. It is what you see first after you start your iMac and are ready to use the computer. It is best thought of as your "work space."

Dialog box A window that appears on the screen to ask you for more information or to confirm an action you wish to take. You must respond to this "computerized questionnaire" before the program will continue. (See *Button* and *Check box.*)

The First Week with My New iMac

Dimmed command A command that is not available to you at this time. It is shown in light gray rather than black.

Disc An alternate spelling for "disk" that usually refers to a CD. (In the interest of consistency, "disk" is used throughout this book.)

Disk A magnetic surface that permanently stores information. The internal hard disk of most computers holds most of your information. Removable disks such as "floppy disks" or "zip disks" are used to back up, or save, data from the hard disk.

Disk drive The mechanism that reads and writes information from and to a disk. There are several types of disk drives: floppy disk drives, hard disk drives, zip disk drives, compact disk drives, etc.

Display Another word for monitor.

Document A file that you create when you save work in an application program.

Domain (and domain name) A means of identifying computers at a location on the Internet. In the United States, the "domain" is the last three letters of an Internet address. It tells you what kind of a group you are communicating with. Examples of domains are: .com (a commercial organization), .org (a non-profit organization), .edu (an educational institution), .gov (part of the U.S. government), and .net (a network). The "domain name" is an easily recognizable name given to a "host" computer rather than using a numerical address.

Double-click To press the left mouse button quickly two times. This is done to select an object or program and open it.

Download To copy files from one computer to another using a network connection. Usually this refers to copying files from the Internet onto your hard drive.

Glossary

Dragging Moving something, such as a folder, by holding down the left mouse button and sliding the mouse over until the object is in the desired position on the screen. It also refers to holding down the mouse button and moving the mouse to highlight a string of text.

Drop-down list A list of items in a dialog box that gives possible alternatives from which to choose.

DVD-ROM An acronym for "Digital Video Disc-Read Only Memory," which refers to a disk that stores data, video images, and audio information. The disk needs a DVD-ROM drive to access this information, and this drive is accessed through the colored slit in the front of the iMac below the screen.

Electronic mail (See *E-mail.*)

E-mail A way of sending messages electronically from one person to another over the Internet or a network. Messages are sent almost instantly and can contain text, files, voice messages, graphics, and photographs. It is a means of communicating around the world at great speed.

Emoticon A set of characters used to visually express an emotion. Also known as "smileys," emoticons are commonly used in e-mail messages.

"esc" key ("escape" key) This key is found on the top row, extreme left side of the keyboard, and is used as a key command to "cancel" an action or to "unfreeze" the computer when all else fails. Pressing the "option" key, the "Command" key, and the "esc" key simultaneously forces the computer to close the frozen program.

Extensions Short last "names" on the end of file names that help identify what program created the file. Examples include: .doc (a Word® document); .tiff (a graphics file); and .jpeg (a file of photos).

The First Week with My New iMac

FAQ The acronym for the words "frequently asked questions."

Field A place in a record for one piece of information.

File A collection of information, such as a document, that is stored on a disk.

File extension (See *Extension*.)

File format (See *Extension*.)

Finder A program that starts automatically when the computer is turned on and that is the graphical user interface that lets you work with all your files, folders, and programs. The Finder *is* the Desktop—it "owns" the Desktop. By clicking on the Finder icon in the top right corner of the Desktop, you can see all the applications or programs that are open and move among them.

Floppy disk A data storage device that is made up of a flexible, round plastic disk encased in a hard plastic case. Most PC floppy disks are 3.5 inches in size and store 1.44 megabytes or 2.88 megabytes of information.

Folder A location on your disk where related files are stored.

Font A complete set of characters that share a specific typeface or appearance. A variety of fonts have been designed since the beginning of the written word. Most word-processing programs will allow you to pick the typeface that you prefer. You can also change fonts within your document if you wish. (See *Typeface*.)

Formatting The process of setting up the font specifications, page layout, and design information for a document.

Function key A set of keys at the top of the keyboard that can be programmed to give specific commands or perform certain tasks. These keys are usually labeled F1 through F12.

Glossary

Gigabyte 1,024 megabytes. The abbreviation for this is GB.

Graphic An image.

Graphical User Interface (GUI) This is pronounced "gooey" and refers to a method that allows computer users to point to icons or pictures on the screen to select files and give commands. Apple Computers developed this easy interface and has always used it.

Hard disk The main storage area for data inside the computer.

Hard disk drive The device that is actually used to store the data and programs in the computer. It consists of sets of magnetically coated disks, called platters, that are stored vertically and rotate up to 3600 rpm. The unit is self-contained and sealed. Storage space on typical hard disk drives now tops 6 to 13 gigabytes and this continues to grow. (**Note:** the terms hard disk, hard disk drive, and hard drive are used interchangeably.)

Hardware A term referring to all the machinery or physical parts of the computer system.

Highlighting A way of marking text or information so that you can make changes to these sections of information when you give the next command. A highlighted section of text appears in contrasting color. Once something is highlighted, it can be cut, pasted, copied, or formatted.

Home page The initial starting page for a World Wide Web site. This page will usually provide an index and links to other pages on the site or to related information on other sites.

Hover To place the cursor over an icon for a short period of time. When this is done, a balloon might appear that describes the function of the icon.

Hypertext Markup Language (HTML) A standardized language used to create pages on the World Wide Web. This language allows browsers to connect or link different pages to each Web site. This is not a "language" you will need to learn, it is just useful to know what the letters mean.

Icon A small picture that represents something, such as files, folders, programs, commands, etc. Pointing the cursor at the picture and pressing the left mouse button gives the computer user access to them.

Inactive window The operating system or the application you are using might display several windows. All of these are "inactive" except for the window with the horizontal gray lines on the title bar. (This is the "active" window.) An inactive window becomes active if you point the cursor somewhere in the window and press the mouse button (click).

Insertion point A blinking vertical line or blinking I-beam cursor that indicates where the next character will appear when you type your next bit of text. It basically is a marker that says "you are here."

Internet The largest computer network in the world. This is a "network of networks" that allows computer users to communicate with each other around the world using e-mail, the World Wide Web, etc. (See Chapter 5.)

Internet Service Provider (ISP) A company or service that connects the individual computer user to the Internet. A fee is usually charged for this service.

Keyboard The set of keys that look like a typewriter and are used to input text, data, and commands into the computer.

Keyboard commands A way of giving menu commands using the keyboard instead of the mouse. It involves pressing down and holding several keys simultaneously and then releasing them. (See Appendix B.)

Glossary

Keyboard shortcuts (See *Keyboard commands.*)

Key combinations (See *Keyboard commands.*)

LAN (See *Local Area Network.*)

Link A way of moving from one bit of information (a word, phrase, or idea) to another within a hypertext document. This information can be in the same or different Internet sites and is accessed through a Web browser. Links are easy to recognize because they are written in blue. The cursor changes to look like a hand when positioned over a link.

Local Area Network (LAN) A group of computers in the same area or place (such as an office) that are all connected. The purpose of a LAN is for people to share files and resources.

Log off (**or Log out**) To disconnect from an Internet Service Provider or computer network by sending a message to terminate the connection. This is also known as "signing off."

Log on (or Log in) To connect to an Internet Service Provider or some other network by entering an identification name or number and password. This is also known as "signing on."

Megabyte 1024 kilobytes, or more than a million bytes. The abbreviation is MB and is pronounced "meg."

Megahertz A measurement of the speed at which a processor works. It is one million cycles per second, and the abbreviation is MHz.

Memory The place where data and programs are kept while they are in use. This is where all processing takes place. Later the information is stored on disks. There are two types of memory. RAM, or random-access memory, allows one to read and write information and change data. Another type of information is ROM, or read-only memory. This

205

The First Week with My New iMac

is information that cannot be changed and is usually used to start and program your computer.

Menu A list of commands that are available in the program with which you are working. By selecting options from the menus, you tell the computer what you want it to do. There are several types of menus: menu bars, pull-down menus, submenus, etc.

Menu bar The row of words on the top of the desktop. These words or names correspond to pull-down menus that allow you to perform different commands.

Microsoft Windows® The operating system used by most PCs. This is the system that simplifies how the computer works so that it manages applications, files, folders, disks, etc., in a "user friendly" way. In the past, PCs used a complicated system of characters to issue all the instructions to the programs. Windows is a graphical operating system that uses icons and pull-down menus to give commands. (See *Graphical User Interface*.)

Modem A piece of electronic hardware that allows a computer to exchange data with another computer over telephone lines.

Monitor The piece of hardware that looks like a television and displays information on a screen.

Motherboard The main circuit board in your computer. It holds the chips that are the central processing unit, memory, etc.

Mouse A device used for pointing on screen that lets you give commands and select items. A mouse usually has one button. Fancier "mice" have at least two buttons on the top. Mouse buttons are pressed once or twice to select and activate commands.

Mouse pointer An icon that is an arrow, a vertical line, a hand, etc., that is controlled by the movement of the mouse. It indicates where you are on the screen or in a window. The pointer allows you to select

Glossary

objects with which you want to work. Another term for the mouse pointer is "cursor."

Network Two or more computers that are connected for the purpose of sharing files, folders, programs, printers, and other resources.

Newsgroup A group of individuals on the Internet who are devoted to discussing a particular topic. Messages are "posted" electronically on a "bulletin board" so that others in the group can read them and respond.

OCR (Optical Character Recognition) Software that takes an optically scanned image and converts it into letters and characters that can be recognized and used in text files by the computer.

Off-line 1) Hardware, such as a printer, that is not in "ready" mode and so is not available for use. 2) The term used when you are not connected to the Internet.

"OK" button An element in the dialog box that allows you to confirm a task. It also can take you to the next level of a program. Often you can press the "return" key instead of clicking on the "OK" button.

On-line 1) Hardware, such as a printer or a modem, that is ready to operate and is connected to a computer. 2) The term used when you are connected to the Internet.

On-line service A service that provides Internet connection and service to its subscribers through a modem. (See *Internet Service Provider.*)

Operating system Software that runs your computer and controls programs and hardware. Mac OS® 9 is an operating system.

Option buttons Small circles that are used in dialog boxes to allow

207

The First Week with My New iMac

you to make a single choice. When only one choice is possible you have the option of clicking this button to turn it on (button is black) or off (button is white).

Path A way of representing a directory or file that shows the location of the item in terms of the computer's filing system. It is a map that names the drive, folders, and files in which the item is located.

PC The acronym for "personal computer." It usually refers to a computer with a Windows operating system. A computer not made by Apple Computer, Inc., is a PC.

Pentium A type of processor that was created by a company called Intel for use in PCs. Currently there are several generations of this processor, including Pentium II and Pentium III.

Peripheral The term for hardware, such as a printer, that is used with a computer.

Personal Computer (See *PC.*)

Pointer (See *Mouse pointer.*)

Processor (See *CPU.*)

Program A set of instructions that tell the computer what to do and how to do it. Programs are software.

Public domain software Software that is not copyrighted, is freely distributed, and can be used or copied by anyone. Other names for this software are "freeware" and "shareware." It is most commonly available over the Internet.

Pull-down menu A hidden, vertical menu that is opened with the menu bar (the bar at the top of the desktop). It allows you to access commands and features of that particular program.

Glossary

Radio buttons (See *Option buttons*.)

RAM (See *Memory*.)

Random Access Memory (See *Memory*.)

Restart To turn off the computer, start it again, and reload the operating system. This procedure is usually performed when the computer freezes or crashes, or after some new software is installed. Most computers have a "Reset" button that will restart the computer without turning off the power. Another way to restart is to go to "Special" on the menu bar and click on "Restart." It is also referred to as "rebooting" the computer.

Save A command that records or transfers your data onto the computer's hard disk for permanent storage. As you enter information it is placed into the computer's memory. Depending on the program you are using, it will be lost if there is a power failure, the computer crashes, there is a program error, or you turn off the machine. It is very important to save your work every few minutes onto the hard drive. Some programs such as Quicken® do save automatically. You should also save information on a floppy disk or zip disk every few days as an additional backup, no matter which program you are using.

Scanner A piece of hardware (peripheral) that lets you copy an image into the computer by changing the optical information to digital information.

Scroll bar A vertical or horizontal bar that appears on the right side and at the bottom of a window when there is more information in the window than can be seen at one time. It allows you to move down or over by clicking and holding down the appropriate arrow buttons to see the rest of the information. A small box within the bar shows you your relative position with respect to the information in the window.

The First Week with My New iMac

SCSI An acronym for "small computer system interface"—pronounced "scuzzy." Its purpose is to connect several pieces of hardware to your computer while only using one port.

Search engines Companies that use sophisticated software to find information on the Internet for computer users. Examples are www.Yahoo.com, www.askjeeves.com, www.lycos.com, and www.excite!.com.

Select To choose an item on a menu or to highlight something. The result is that some action will take place with the next command you give.

Server A computer that provides files, data, and other services to a network of computers. These other computers are called clients.

Shareware Software that is provided over the Internet free of charge for a trial period. If you continue to use the program you are asked to pay a fee. (See *Public domain software*.)

Sherlock® 2 This is your new best friend. Sherlock is a program on the Mac OS® 9 operating system that searches and finds anything you want. It can find files on the hard drive or information from the Internet.

Shortcut A special icon that points to or represents another program, folder, file, etc., that is still in its original location on the hard drive. The icon sits on your desktop and allows you quick access to the program or information without taking up extra space. You can recognize these special icons by the little arrow in their lower left corner. (See *Alias*.)

Shortcut keys Keys or combinations of keys that are used to give commands. They provide another way of asking the computer to perform some action when you do not want to use the mouse pointer to select and click a command from a menu or icon. Using shortcut keys is usually a faster way to give a command. (See *Keyboard commands*.)

Shut down The proper way to turn off the computer and cut off its power supply. Go to the word "Special" on the menu bar; the bottom option is "Shut Down." If you select "Shut Down" the computer is turned off.

Sleep A way that the computer saves energy by shutting off the monitor and winding down the hard drive in such a way that it is not totally turned off. If nothing is done on the computer for a fixed number of minutes it will go to sleep by itself. If you want to put it to sleep then go to "Special" on the menu bar and click on "Sleep." To "wake-up" the computer, press any key. (See last question in Appendix A, Troubleshooting.) Also note how the color of the power button on the monitor changes from green to amber when the machine is "asleep" and fades in and out as if it were snoring!

Software The term that is used to describe programs, operating systems, applications, etc. Basically if it is visible and a piece of equipment, it is hardware. If it is invisible and coded information that runs the computer, it is software.

Sound board (**sound card**) A circuit board that changes program instructions into high-quality sound. Most programs today are multimedia and take advantage of a sound board. Sound boards also make it possible for you to listen to your favorite audio CD while you work at your computer.

Startup disk A floppy disk or CD that holds all the operating system information. This is used to reboot your computer if the hard drive malfunctions.

Surfing To browse the Internet. To surf means to move from one topic of interest to another while you are connected to the World Wide Web. Some people spend hours going from one link to another. (See Appendix F.)

Surge protector A device used to regulate the electrical power that goes into the computer. It prevents electrical spikes or surges from

The First Week with My New iMac

damaging the computer. It is plugged into the electrical outlet, and the power cord of the computer is plugged into the surge protector.

System board (See *Motherboard*.)

System Folder A folder on the hard drive that holds everything that is needed by the operating system to run the computer. It includes utilities, programs, and files.

Tab This is found in dialog boxes and is similar to the tabs on folders that you keep in your filing cabinet. Just as with your files, these tabs are labeled. When selected they give a number of options corresponding to the name of that folder.

"tab" key When using a word-processing program, this key inserts tabs just as it does on a typewriter. When using other applications, where it is necessary to fill in data, this key moves the cursor from one "field" to the next. For example, when sending e-mail via America Online, you can use the "tab" key to move from the "Send To" field to the "Subject" field to the field where you enter your message. It is easier than pointing the cursor to a field and clicking.

Title bar The horizontal bar at the top of each window that contains the name of the window (such as the application or file name) on which you are working. It also shows the Collapse box, the Zoom box, and the Close box. When a window is active, the title bar is gray with horizontal lines and black letters.

Tool bar (See *Button Bar*.)

Trash This is your wastepaper basket or garbage can. The Trash holds all the data that you have deleted. It is visible on the desktop as an icon that looks like its namesake. As with all icons, if you double-click on this icon, it will open and you can view the contents. If you "empty" the Trash, all the information is gone permanently.

Glossary

Type size This is a measurement that tells the height of a font. It is traditionally measured in "points." The type size that you are using in a text document is shown below the button bar.

Type style This refers to the effects that you can use to change the appearance of your text such as **bold**, *italic*, and underline. Either the button in the middle of the button bar or key commands are used to change type style.

Typeface The common design characteristics of a group of letters, numbers, and symbols. The typeface is also known as the font, and you can see which one you are using in a text document by looking at the left side of the format bar. (See *Font*.)

URL (**Universal Resource Locator**) Another term for an address on the Internet. It is a series of characters that connect you to a specific site on the World Wide Web.

USB (**Universal Serial Bus**) The standard type of connection or interface between the different peripherals, such as the mouse and keyboard, and the computer. USBs allow you to plug in hardware and use it right away without restarting. The iMac comes with four USB ports.

Virus Software that is designed to damage your computer or files without your knowledge. Sometimes viruses are simple pranks, and sometimes they are meant to destroy entire systems. Viruses are usually passed from one program or file to another through "infected" floppy disks you may receive, or by downloading something off the Internet that may be tainted. Some viruses can wipe out all the information stored on a hard disk. This is the reason you should back up your data on floppy disks or zip disks. In addition, you can install anti-virus software that will scan everything coming into your computer.

Web (See *World Wide Web*.)

The First Week with My New iMac

Web browser (See *Browser.*)

Window The rectangle on your screen that shows a program or application and the data, file, or folder on which you are working. You can have several windows visible and open on your desktop simultaneously. However, only one window is active at a time.

Windows This refers to the operating system of personal computers (as in Windows 98®) that was developed by the company called Microsoft®. (See *Operating system; Microsoft Windows®.*)

Word-processing software A program or application that allows you to use the computer as a typewriter. It manages text so that you can write, format, edit, and store documents. Examples of word-processing programs include AppleWorks®, Microsoft Word®, and Corel WordPerfect®.

World Wide Web A portion of the Internet that connects graphical and multimedia information (words, pictures, video, and sound). On the Web you can move from one site to another with the aid of a browser. (See *Internet; Browser; Link.*)

WYSIWYG An acronym for "what you see is what you get." It is pronounced "wizzy-wig." Programs that can show you on the screen exactly how they will look when printed out are called "wysiwyg."

Zip disk (See *Zip drive.*)

Zip drive A disk drive that uses disks that are physically similar in size to floppy disks but hold much more data. A zip disk can store 100 megabytes of data.

Zoom Box A button on the top right side of the title bar that increases the size of a window so that it fills the screen. When the window is already full size, clicking on the same button (which looks like two overlapping windows) will restore the window to its original size.

Index

The First Week with My New iMac

Figures are indicated by an italicized *f* following the page number where the figure appears.

(). See Apple key
(⌘). See Command key
(⏻). See power symbol, universal

abbreviations (in E-mail), 187
ABC icon, 86
access, quick
    desktop folders, 138–139*f*
    to documents, 118–119
    to programs, 167
active programs, 169
active tabs, 21
active windows, 15, 168
activities, computer, 4
addiction to computer, 192
Address Book
    adding names, 130–131*f*
    selecting names, 58, 127–128
addresses. *See* E-mail addresses; Web addresses
alias, creating, 118–119, 138–139*f*
All Things Considered (NPR), 175
Altavista (search engine), 72
alternative medicine, web addresses for, 181
alt (alternate) key, 23
America Online (AOL)
    closing, 72
    connecting to, 48–52, 123
    E-mail (*See* E-mail)
    installing with CD, 60
    local news/information, 44–45
    movie listings, 44
    My Places, 64*f*, 66, 69
    My Portfolios, 65–69
    My Weather, 63, 64*f*
    signing on, 50–52
    surfing the Internet, 44–45, 69–72
'any' key, 176
AOL. See America On Line (AOL)
Apple Computer Company, contact information, 188
Apple key (), 23, 23*f*. *See also* keyboard commands

Index

Apple menu, 19*f*
    Control Panel, 18–22, 19*f*, 136–137
    opening, 136
    Stickies, 98
AppleWorks
    ABC icon, 86
    accidental deletions, 170
    AppleWorks 5 alias, 81
    backing up to disk, 154–155
    bolding/italicizing/underlining, 89–90, 93*f*, 147–148, 171
    button bar of, 83*f*, 166
    creating new document, 92, 94–98
    cutting and pasting, 92
    font, changing, 90–91*f*, 148–151*f*, 171–172
    formatting, 88–92, 93*f*
    insertion point, 34*f*
    justifying text, 89
    letter writing, 83–93
    menu bar of, 83*f*
    naming untitled document, 95
    no automatic save feature, 80
    opening, 81–83, 82*f*
    page numbering, 171
    printing, 142, 152-153*f*
    removing icons, 166
    resizing pages, 171
    rulers, 94
    saving work, 80, 92, 94–98, 142–143*f*
    spell checking, 85–88, 87*f*
    symbols, 23
    templates, 27, 143–145
    typing, 82, 83*f*
    Undo command, 39–40, 170
    wrap around text, 22
    Writing Tools, 86, 87*f*
arrow keys, 24
    highlighting with, 39
    uses, 38
Askjeeves (search engine), 72
audio CDs, listening to, 103, 157–158
author's E-mail address, 4

back arrow on web browser, 71
backing up files to floppy disk, 110, 154–155. *See also* saving work
backspacing, with delete key, 24, 85
balloons, activating/deactivating, 16, 166, 169

217

The First Week with My New iMac

Barnes and Noble on the Web, 71
bifocals, 191
binging/bonging noises, 11, 112, 168
blank 'paper'
    for new document, 82, 92, 94
    for new E-mail message, 54–55*f*, 127
blank screen, 164
blue, underlined text, 71
Blue Mountain Cards on the Web, 71
bolding, 89–90, 93*f*, 147–148, 171
bookmarks, marking, 69
books
    computer, 105, 176
    electronic, 160–162
    web addresses for, 182
booting, 112
brightness, adjusting, 115, 117*f*
brokerage statements, 67
browsers. *See* surfing the net
bundled software, 99
button bar (AppleWorks), 83f
    removing buttons, 166
buying on-line, 183

cables, 6, 108–109
canceling a task, 164
cancel/OK, escape key, 23*f*, 24
capital letters, in E-mail, 186
cards, electronic greeting, 71
Carpal Tunnel Syndrome, 189–191*f*
CD disk drives. *See* disk drives
CD-ROM. *See* Glossary
CDs
    additional games, 7
    audio, 103, 157–158
    loading/unloading, 102–103, 110–111
chairs, height of, 189–191*f*
clicking
    to open programs, 15
    right button, 172
    single vs. double, 165–166
 triple clicking, 88, 147
clicking and dragging
    moving icons, 14
    moving solitaire cards, 74–76

Index

clipboard, cutting and pasting, 92
clock, setting, 116
closing dialogue boxes, 173
closing windows, 15–16, 120
Command key (⌘), 23–24. *See also* keyboard commands
    Command, shift, or option key, 174–175
compact disks. *See* CDs
computer information, web addresses for, 183–184
computer literacy, 54
computers, iMac
    customizing options, 7
    initial set up, 9–12, 108–109
    keeping a notebook, 27–28
    overcoming fear of, 32–33
    pre-purchasing, 5–8
    registering, 25
    space for, 3
    technical support, 188
    turning on/off, 11–12, 111–113*f*
computer skills, practicing, 2, 14–15, 73
computer tables, 10
connectors, female/male, 108
contrast, adjusting, 115, 117*f*
control key, 23
controllers
    CD, 158*f*
    DVD-CD, 100, 159
Control Panel, 19*f*, 116*f*, 136–137
    changing display, 20–21
    changing mouse properties, 20, 115–116, 117*f*
    changing settings, 114–118
    enlarging icons, 114
Control Strip, 17*f*–18, 136–137
copying text, 92, 172
Corel WordPerfect, 80
    tech support, 188
correspondence. *See* documents
crash, computer, 32
creating
    E-mail (*See* E-mail)
    new document, 82–83, 92, 94–98
    new folders, 96–97*f*
    stock portfolios, 65–69, 134–135*f*
    templates, 143–145
cursor
    changing speed, 20, 26*f*, 115–116, 115–116*f*, 117*f*
    at insertion point, 12–13

219

moving with arrow key, 38
moving with tab key, 58
possible shapes of, 12–13, 34
customizing options, computers, iMac, 7
cutting and pasting, 92

date and time adjustments, 116, 116f, 119f
delete key, 23f, 24, 85
deletions, reversing, 39–40, 170
desktop
    arranging icons, 14
    changing appearance, 20–22, 136–137, 173
    definition, 28–29
    icons, identifying, 167
    placing folders on, 97–98f, 118–119, 138–139f
    resolution, 18
dialogue boxes
    closing, 173
    using tab key between, 58
disk drives
    installing external, 109, 110
    types of, 6
disks, 7
documents. See also AppleWorks
    creating new, 92, 94–98, 140–142f, 143f
    formatting, 147–151
    printing, 142, 152–153f
    quick access to, 118–119
    saving, 92, 94–95f, 97f, 142–143f
document type, save as, 97
domain names, 42, 70, 72
double clicking, 15
    unresponsive icon, 165
    vs. single, 165
downloading games, 74
dragging. See clicking and dragging
drives. See disk drives
drop down menus, opening, 36, 94f
DVD-CDs (DVD-Movies)
    loading/viewing, 100
    no automatic start, 168
    playing, 158–159
    renting over Internet, 100, 182

Index

e-Books, 160–162
Edit menu, 39, 87*f*
educational websites, 180
    domain names for, 43
ejecting CDs, 103, 111
    using paper clip, 168
E-mail
    addresses (*See* Address Book; E-mail addresses)
    common abbreviations, 187
    composing new, 127–128
    deleting mail, 59–60
    forwarding messages, 56–57, 58, 125–126, 126*f*
    group mailings, 131
    junk mail, 59
    Mail Center, 59
    multiple recipients, 58
    Online Mailbox, 52–53*f*
    reading messages, 52–54
    receiving, 123–124
    replying to, 54–57, 124–125, 126*f*
    Send Later, 56, 57*f*
    Send Now, 56, 57*f*
    Send To, 55, 57
    Smileys, 186
    storing received mail, 59
    Subject box (AOL), 51, 57
    tutorial, 54
    waiting to be sent, 129–130, 129*f*
    Welcome window, 52–53*f*
E-mail addresses
    author's, 4
    parts of, 43
    @ symbol, 43
    your address, 60–61
emoticons, 186
Encarta Encyclopedia, 100
encyclopedias
    installing, 100–101
    online, web addresses for, 180
    using, 101–103
enter key, 38
Eric'xxs Solitaire. *See* solitaire
esc (escape) key, 24
exercise and your computer, 190–191*f*
eyeglasses, monitor distance, 191

The First Week with My New iMac

Favorites, marking, 69
File menu
    creating new folders, 138–139
    Save As, 94–95*f*
file names
    choosing, 95
    length of, 172
financial information
    using My Portfolios, 65–69, 134–135*f*
    web addresses for, 183
Finder icon, 17
finding
    lost files/folders, 104
    people, on the web, 180
First Week with My New PC, The, 164
Fitness Link, web address, 181
flaming (in E-mail), 186
floppy disk drives. *See* disk drives
floppy disks, backing up files, 110, 154–155
folders
    creating aliases, 118–119, 138–139*f*
    creating new, 95f, 97, 138–139*f*
    labeling, 140
    levels, moving between, 96, 97*f*, 167
    moving, 140
    opening, 34–35, 120
    saving to, 96
    saving to automatically, 146
fonts
    changing size, 91f, 149–150, 151*f*
    changing style, 89–90
    changing system fonts, 136–137
    changing typeface, 90–91*f*, 148–149
format bar, 83
forward arrow on web browser, 71
forwarding E-mail, 56–58, 125–126*f*
frames. *See* windows
freezing, 32
    restarting, 137
    ways to correct, 174

games. *See also* solitaire
    downloading, 74
    other card games, 7, 77, 156–157
Glossary, 193–214

Index

greeting cards, electronic, 71
grounded outlets, 109

hand shaped cursor, 34, 70–71, 76
hardware, definition, 6
health
    addictive computer behavior, 192
    bifocals, 191
    ergonomics, 189–191*f*
    exercises, 190–191*f*
health directories and organizations, web addresses for, 180–181
help
    hiring experts, 22
    setting up computer, 10
    unwanted, 173–174
Help Center, 17, 17*f*
Help menu, desktop, 16–17
hidden windows, 169
highlighting
    individual lines, 147
    paragraphs, 90
    single words, 85, 147
    unhighlighting, 146
    unintentionally, 165
    using shift and arrow keys, 39
    ways to, 88
    whole document, 147
home pages
    bookmarking, 69
    getting to, 70
horizontal scroll bar, 38*f*

icon bar, 35*f*
icons
    balloon descriptors, 16, 166, 169
    definition, 28, 28*f*, 166
    enlarging, 114
    moving, 14
    shaded, 165
iMovie, 103–104, 159
insertion point, 34*f*
    cursor appearance, 12–13
    making corrections, 85–86

Internet. *See also* surfing the net; Web addresses
    getting on to, 132–133*f*
    kinds of information on, 44–45
    organization of, 42–43
    renting DVD movies through, 100
    shopping on, 183
Internet addiction, 192
Internet Service Providers (ISPs). *See also* America Online (AOL)
    choices, and trial periods, 48, 60
    connecting to, 122–123
    setting up, 60
ISPs. *See* Internet Service Providers (ISPs)
italicizing, 89–90, 93*f*, 147–148, 171

jacks, telephone, 10, 109
junk mail, 59
justifying text, 89

keyboard commands, 36–37
    combined with mouse commands, 172
    Command key, 23–24
    list of, 177–178
keyboards, 23*f*
    ergonomic, 7, 189
    initial installation, 108
    key functions, 22–24
    proper height for, 189
    USB connection on, 110
keyword searches, 70

labeling, folders, 140
Landau, Ted, 105
Langer, Maria, 105
letter writing. *See also* documents
    examples, 84, 93
Linking Human Systems, 192
links, 71, 105
listening to audio CDs, 103, 157–158
literacy, computer, 54
loading CDs, 102–103, 110
logging on to AOL, 50–52
lost files/folders, finding, 104
Lycos (search engine), 72

Index

Macintosh HD, 49f
    opening AppleWorks, 81, 82f
    opening Internet folder, 49
MAC OS 9, 105
Mailbox (AOL), 53f
Mail Center, 59
maps, sources
    web addresses for, 181
    World Book Encyclopedia, 101
menu bars, 16, 17, 35f
    AppleWorks, 83f
Metropolitan Opera on the Web, 71
Microsoft Reader, 160
Microsoft Word, 80
mistakes
    spelling errors, 86–88
    typing errors, 85–88, 87f
    Undo command, 39–40, 170
modems
    connecting to telephone, 109
    dialing an ISP, 51–52
modifier keys, 174–175
monitors
    changing settings, 18, 115, 117f
    power cords, 108
    troubleshooting, 164
mouse. *See also* cursor, clicking
    ball in, 13
    basic usage, 7, 12–15
    changing settings, 115–116, 117f
    iMac tutorial, 14
    initial installation, 108
    single vs. multi button, 172
    'tail' of, 12, 33
movie listings
    web addresses for, 182
    web searches for, 44
music, web addresses for, 182
My Documents, 27
My Places (AOL)
    Change My Places, 69
    Set My Places, 64f, 65, 69
My Portfolios (AOL), create/set up, 65–69, 134–135f
My Weather (AOL), 63, 64f

The First Week with My New iMac

naming
    documents, 94, 95*f*, 172
    folders, 138
    your computer, 32, 192
National Public Radio (NPR), 175–176
new documents, creating, 82–83, 92, 93–94
new folders, creating, 95*f*, 96–97*f*
news on the web, 179–180
Northernlight (search engine), 72
notebooks, keeping, 27–28
notes, writing, 98
nothing works, 32, 174

Online Mailbox (AOL), 52, 53*f*
online shopping, 182–183
on/off button, 11, 111
operating system (OS), software compatibility, 7
Options, (solitaire), 74
option key, 23, 174–175

paper clips, to eject CDs, 168
passwords, for ISP account, 50
pasting, cutting and, 92
payments over the web, 183
PC vs. iMac computers, 164
peripherals, definition, 6
pointer. *See* cursor
ports
    identifying, 11
    plugging into, 108–109, 110
postage services, web addresses, 180
power management, 29, 111–113*f*, 164
power symbol, universal (⏻), 11, 111
practicing
    with mouse, 14–15
    necessity of, 2
    by playing games, 73
preferences. *See* settings
previous page, 71
printer cables, 6, 10
    attaching, 108
printer icon, 83, 92
printers, 6
    installing, 109

Index

printing
    documents, 142, 152–153*f*
    preview, 152
programs, opening, 120
pull down menus. *See* drop down menus

questions, writing down, 27–28
quick access
    desktop folders, 138–139*f*
    to documents, 118–119
    to programs, 167
Quicken, 67
quotes, stock market, 65–69, 134–135*f*

radio shows, on Internet, 175–176
rebooting, 113
records, keeping a notebook, 27–28
reference guides
    computer books, 105, 164
    encyclopedias, 100–103
    online, 104
    web addresses for, 180
resetting, 174
resolution (monitor), 18, 115, 117f
restarting computer, 112–113*f*, 137
restaurants, web addresses for, 181–182
return key, 22, 23*f*, 38
right clicking, 172

Sad Macs, Bombs, and Other Disasters, 105
Save As, 94–95*f*
saving work
    automatically to folder, 146
    backing up to floppy disk, 154–155
    File menu, 94*f*
    in folders, 95f, 96–98
    importance of, 80, 110
    length of file names, 172
    mouse/keyboard commands, 94, 145
    Save As, 94–95*f*
scissors icon, 92, 170
scroll bars, 38
scrolling (mouse technique), 21, 121

search engines, 72, 133*f*
  list of, 179
  using Sherlock 2, 104–105, 133, 133*f*
Search words, 70–71
secure sites, 183
Send Later (AOL), 56, 57*f*, 128, 129–130
Send Now (AOL), 56, 57*f*, 128
Send To (AOL), 55
  adding names, 127–128
Set My Places, 64*f*, 65
settings
  changing in Control Panel, 18–22, 19*f*, 114–118, 136
  changing on Control Strip, 17–18, 136
set up
  ISP account, 60
  new computer, 9–12, 108–109
shaded icons, 165
shaded windows, 168–169
Sherlock 2, 104–105, 133, 133*f*
shift key
  command, shift, or option key, 174–175
  highlighting with, 88, 90, 146
shopping on the web, websites and payment tips, 182–184
shortcuts. *See* alias; keyboard commands
shouting (in E-mail), 186
shutting off the computer
  how to, 112–113*f*, 137
  when to, 29
Sign On (AOL), 50f, 51
Simple Text, 82
single clicking, vs. double, 165–166
sleep mode, 29, 112–113*f*
  waking up, 164
'snail' mail, 60
Snap (search engine), 72
software
  bundled, 99
  definition, 6
  OS compatibility, 7
software companies, web addresses for, 188
solitaire
  game board, 37*f*, 76f
  installation CD, 74
  instructions, 74, 76
  keyboard commands, 37, 76

Index

    moving the cards, 74–76
    playing, 75–77, 76f, 155–156
sound. *See also* sounds, system
    adjusting volume, 18, 158
sounds, system
    binging or bonging, 11, 112, 168
    changing, 136–137
Special menu
    ejecting CDs, 110–111
    power management options, 113f, 137
Spell Check
    ABC icon, 86
    keyboard/mouse commands, 86
    methods, 85–88, 87f
sports, web addresses for, 182
starting the computer, 11–12, 111–112
Stickies, 98
stock market
    creating My Portfolios, 65–69, 134–135f
    following on AOL, 134–135
stopping tasks, 164
stretching, periodically, 190–191f
Style drop down menu, 89f
Subject box (AOL), 55
surfing the net
    connecting to AOL, 48–52
    favorite sites, 69
    finding information, 43–45, 69–72
    using forward/backward arrows, 71
surge protectors, 10
    definition, 7
    plugging into, 109
symbols, 23
System Folder, 20–22

tab (tabulation) key, 24
    moving cursor with, 58
tax information, web addresses for, 183
technical support
    contact information, 188
    most asked question, 176
telephone calls, while 'on-line,' 51
telephone jacks, connecting to, 10, 109
templates, 27
    creating, 143–145

text. *See* documents
thesaurus tool, 86
tickets, web addresses for, 181
time and date adjustments, 116, 136–137
title bar, 15f, 35f
    AppleWorks, 83*f*
toggling, 21
Trash can
    emptying, 167
    retrieving from, 168
travel information, web addresses for, 181
triple clicking, highlighting by, 88, 147
troubleshooting
    active windows/programs, 168, 169
    'any' key, 176
    balloons, activating/deactivating, 169
    beeping/binging, 168
    blank screen, 164
    clicking, double vs. single, 165–166
    command, shift, or option key, 174–175
    desktop
        backgrounds, 173
        icons on, 167
    file names, 172
    fonts, changing, 171–172
    'frozen' computer, 174
    icons
        desktop, 167
        identifying, 166, 167
        removing, 166
        unresponsive, 165
    inactive windows/programs, 169
    keyboard commands and mouse clicks, 172
    lines/numbers at bottom of screen, 171
    mouse envy, 172
    no autostart on DVD-CDs, 168
    nothing makes sense, 164
    nothing works, 32, 174
    right clicking, 172
    saving work, 171
    stopping a task, 164
    text, disappearing, 170
    Trash can
        emptying, 167
        retrieving from, 168

Index

        underlining/italicizing/bolding, 171
        undoing mistakes, 39–40, 170
        unwanted help, 173–174
        VCRs, 176
        web addresses, 175–176
        windows, closing, 173
tutorials
        connecting to Internet, 122–124
        Desktop Skills (mouse), 14
        E-mail (AOL), 54
        iMovie, 103–104, 159
typeface, selecting fonts, 90–91*f*, 148–149

underlining, 89–90, 93*f*, 147–148, 171
Undo command, 39–40, 170
unhighlighting, 146
unknown web addresses, 72
untitled documents, naming, 94–95*f*
USB ports, 108, 110
user names, 43

VCRs, 176
vertical scroll bar, 38*f*
videos, editing, 103–104
viruses/worms, 80
volume, adjusting, 18, 19*f*, 158

weather information, 63, 64*f*, 179
        web searches for, 43–44
Web addresses
        domain name of, 42
        guessing tips, 71
        interesting sites, 179–185
        locating sites, 70–72
        troubleshooting, 45
Web Addresses of Interest, 179–185
web browser. See surfing the net
Welcome window (AOL), 70*f*. *See also* E-mail
        financial portfolios, 65–69, 134-135*f*
        local news/information, 63–64
        My Places (AOL), 69

The First Week with My New iMac

windows
    active vs. shaded, 168–69
    closing all, 173
    hidden, 169
    moving, 120
    opening/closing, 15–16, 120, 121–122f, 173
    resizing, 120–121
    scrolling, 21, 38, 121
word counter, 86
word processing programs, 80. *See also* AppleWorks
World Book Encyclopedia
    finding information, 101
    installing, 100–101, 102f
    quitting, 102–103
wrap around text, 22
www, 45, 70
WYSIWYG, 5

Yahoo (search engine), 72
"You've Got Mail" (AOL), 52

zip disk drives. *See* disk drives

Golden Mouse Award

This "Golden Mouse" certificate has been awarded to iMac Master,

_____
[your name]

in recognition of completion of your "first week with your new iMac" spent comprehending and accomplishing the skills of diligent unboxing, complicated machinery set-up, and mastering of software, keyboard keys, computer games, email correspondence with friends and family, Internet surfing, CD listening, and generally "getting connected" to the new world of personal computing.

Officially awarded this ____ day of _____ month in the year of _____,

Authorized by

Pamela R. Lessing
Pamela R. Lessing, "First Week" Counselor